Combermere School and the Barbadian Society

Cartoon of the staff sketched by Frank Collymore in 1935.

COMBERMERE SCHOOL AND THE BARBADIAN SOCIETY

By

Keith A. P. Sandiford
and
Earle H. Newton

BARBADOS • JAMAICA • TRINIDAD AND TOBAGO

The Press University of the West Indies
1A Aqueduct Flats Mona
Kingston 7 Jamaica W I

© 1995 by Keith A. Sandiford & Earle H. Newton
All rights reserved. Published 1995
Printed in the United States of America
ISBN 976-640-014-8

99 98 97 96 95   5 4 3 2 1

CATALOGUING IN PUBLICATION DATA

Sandiford, Keith A.
    Combermere School and the Barbadian society / Keith A.
Sandiford and Earle H. Newton.

    p. cm.
    Includes bibliographical references.
    ISBN 976-640-014-8
    1. Combermere School (Barbados).
    2. Education, Secondary—Barbados—History.
    I. Newton, Earle H. II. Title.
    LE17.B3S36 1995   374.972981

Set in 12/14pt Adobe Garamond
Book design by Prodesign Ltd.
This book has been printed on acid-free paper

This book is dedicated to the memory and honour of Major Cecil Noott, Jack Adams, Frank Collymore, Lionel Gitteus and Chalmer St Hill, and to the honour of Gladstone Holder, Ronnie Hughes and Harry Sealy, all of whom have made a tremendous contribution to Combermere School. Each in his own way and in different measure has been instrumental in the development and education of the authors.

Contents

List of illustrations   *ix*
Preface   *xi*

Chapter One
Combermere's First Two Hundred Years:
The Roots of a Great School   *1*

Chapter Two
The Role of George Bishop Richardson Burton   *23*

Chapter Three
Combermere School, 1926-46:
Twenty Years of Rapid Growth   *48*

Chapter Four
The Age of Noott, 1946-61   *69*

Chapter Five
Consolidation at Waterford, 1961-81   *103*

Chapter Six
Combermere School Since 1981   *122*

Chapter Seven
Epilogue   *139*

Notes   *149*
Select Bibliography   *166*
Index   *171*

List of Illustrations

1. Lord Combermere, after whom the School was named	5
2. Rev. T. Lyall Speed, Headmaster 1879–96	21
3. G.B.R. Burton, Headmaster 1897–1925	24
4. G.B.R. Burton, staff and Student Body in 1910, near the School on Constitution Hill	32
5. Rev. A.E. Armstrong, Headmaster 1934–46	56
6. Cartoon of the staff sketched by Frank Collymore in 1935	57
7. Division 1 Cricket Champions, 1940–41	62
8. Combermere School Cadet Corps, camping in Grenada 1939	63
9. Rev. A.E. Armstrong and his staff, 1942	66
10. Major C.E. Noott, Headmaster 1946–61	70
11. The canteen at Weymouth, 1944–55	82
12. The Hockey XI in 1960	92
13. Major C.E. Noott and members of the CSOBA, 1946	98
14. The staff, 1967–68	108
15. C.W. Pilgrim, Headmaster 1981–86	132
16. The Principal, K.A. Roach, preparing to celebrate the School's 300th anniversary	136
17. Frank Collymore who served the School for many years	141

Preface

The research for this book on Combermere School, our alma mater proceeded in earnest, even though in fits and starts (and with many more of the former than the latter), from 1985. It was much facilitated by the wholehearted cooperation and encouragement of the Combermere School Board of Management, its alumni and its staff. Mr George Belgrave, a former chairman of the Board, and Mr Charles Pilgrim, then headmaster, were extremely supportive. They allowed us full and free access to the Combermere School Records at Waterford during the summer months of 1985, 1986 and 1987. The present headmaster, Mr Keith Roach, has also been very cooperative and provided invaluable information and insights. So too did Major Noott before his death in February 1992. Mrs Dorien Pile, the deputy principal, who has been teaching at the school since 1967 not only provided information and insightful comments but also critically reviewed most of the chapters.

The project has also been encouraged by the Combermere School Old Scholars' Association and Mr Basil Levine, in particular, has been urging us to complete it. Another old Combermerian, Mr David Williams, a member of the staff at the Department of National Archives in Black Rock, has also been most helpful indeed.

The study has profited enormously from the willingness of the Combermere staff and alumni to be interviewed. It has also been enriched by the editorial advice of such colleagues as Professors John Finlay, John Kendle and Edward Moulton of the University of Manitoba and Professor Hilary Beckles of the University of the West Indies. Nor could it have been brought to fruition without the contributions also of Ms Karen Morrow of the University of

Manitoba and Ms Lucia Lewis of the University of the West Indies, who helped us unravel the mysteries of Wordperfect 5.1.

There have, however, been numerous obstacles. While fairly substantial records appear for the years when G.B.Y. Cox (1926-34) and Noott (1946-61) administered the school, there are significantly fewer of them for other periods. We found this particularly baffling for the 1960s and 1970s, when there could be no good reason for the disappearance or loss of significant documents. Many of the records relating to the Burton and Armstrong administrations were apparently lost during the flood of 1949 and the hurricane of 1955. Some records were destroyed or abandoned when the school was effecting its various moves in 1944, (Constitution Hill to Weymouth), 1955 (to the Drill Hall), and 1958 (to its present location at Waterford). Chronic shortage of space on Constitution Hill also led to the periodical discarding of old documents for which the headmasters felt there was no longer an urgent need. Fortunately, there were several contemporaries willing to testify about the later periods, and of these by far the most helpful was Frank 'Froggie' Gibbons, who had collected a fair body of information about Combermere and was himself planning to write a history of the school. He allowed us full access to his memoirs, notebooks and memorabilia and made a number of perceptive observations when we interviewed him in 1986. Unfortunately, 'Froggie' died before we could complete the project, which he very keenly wanted to see.

The period which has suffered the most from the loss or misplacement of documents is, naturally, the first two hundred years of the school's existence. Now that the vestry records for the eighteenth and nineteenth centuries have been closed to the public, we are left to depend on the results of Harold Hutchinson's research. Hutchinson had been a member of the Combermere School staff from 1916 to 1936. He made good use of available materials when he pieced together the origins of the school for the benefit of the readers of the *Combermerian* during the 1930s. He continued his research on the school long after he had resigned from its staff. Chapters 1 and 2 owe a great deal to the endeavours of Gibbons and Hutchinson.

In writing a text such as this, it is inevitable that persons (alive or dead) who have played an important role in the development of some aspect of the institution may have been overlooked. We do apologize for this wherever it may occur but we must stress that wherever names have been mentioned it was intended to be illustrative and not exhaustive.

Not much has thus far been published on Barbadian education or Barbadian schools. This book will therefore help to fill a gaping void. It is the first of its kind since F.A. Hoyos produced a brief history of the Lodge School from 1745 to 1945 to celebrate that institution's two hundredth anniversary. Hopefully, it will inspire others to write the history of other famous schools and colleges which have played key roles in the education of our cultural, intellectual and political leaders.

The basic aims and objectives of this study are straightforward. The book is intended to throw light on the evolution of one of the most famous academic institutions in the West Indies and to analyze its contribution to the development of modern Barbadian society. It provides a careful analysis of the role of the various headmasters because each administrator, in his own way, helped the school to evolve in keeping with developments taking place around it. If nothing else, the study demonstrates how Combermere was able to keep pace with the socio-political changes occurring in Barbados over the past three hundred years. It evolved from an elementary school for poor whites, or 'redlegs' (as they came to be called) into a first-rate secondary school for all segments of the Barbadian society. That its students and teachers eventually became almost exclusively Black is simply a reflection of the ethnic composition of the community itself. No deliberate attempts were ever made to exclude non-Blacks from Combermere. The school's flexibility, in fact, has been the source of its everlasting fame and popularity. By being consistently more progressive than its counterparts, the school succeeded in making enormously significant contributions to Barbadian life and culture.

Combermere School and the Barbadian Society is essentially a case study. It makes no pretension of comparing the Combermere experience with that of other schools in the old British empire or even within the Caribbean region. Such comparisons would have entailed the manipulation of more empirical data than is currently available. Apart from the Lodge School, no other academic institution, so far as we know, has yet been investigated in the manner in which Combermere is being examined here. Our study, then, has to be viewed as a pioneering effort suffering from all of the disadvantages that attend such enterprises.

Keith A.P. Sandiford
Department of History, University of Manitoba, Winnipeg, Canada

Earle H. Newton
Faculty of Education, University of the West Indies, Cave Hill, Barbados

AUGUST 1994

Combermere School and the Barbadian Society

Chapter One

COMBERMERE'S FIRST TWO HUNDRED YEARS: THE ROOTS OF A GREAT SCHOOL

Combermere School is one of the oldest academic institutions in the Commonwealth. Its roots go back as far as the seventeenth century when public education had not yet become the norm, even in Great Britain itself. Combermere's origins are to be found in the will of Colonel Henry Drax, son of Sir James Drax, the famous Roundhead, who had been one of the original planters in Barbados and had established the substantial Drax Hall estate in the parish of St George. Colonel Drax died in London in September 1683, leaving a considerable sum from his private fortune to found a free school in Bridgetown, St Michael, for poor white children. He was also hoping for £20,000 from the various vestries to make the plan viable.[1]

Drax's decision to establish a sizeable fund for the education of poor white youths in Barbados was totally in keeping with the behaviour and attitudes of contemporary Barbadian benefactors, who felt that poor Whites should be trained for clerical positions which the society believed that the Blacks were incapable of occupying. This emphasis on education therefore had a practical as well as racial basis. There was an urgent need on the sugar plantations for bookkeepers, secretaries, managers, overseers and foremen. As these positions were generally beneath the dignity of the wealthy landowners, a white bourgeoisie had to be artificially manufactured and specially trained. Most of the Caribbean planters of that period sincerely believed that, for the sake of social and organic harmony, a clear distinction had to be made between races as well as classes. It would therefore have been most inappropriate to leave poor white families in the same inferior condition as the few Blacks and Mulattoes who had been recently manumitted.

This point has to be emphasized because it can otherwise be assumed that the drive towards public education was an integral part of an overall liberal programme designed to profit all segments of the Barbadian society. In fact, there was nothing particularly democratic or liberal about the decisions reached by benefactors such as Christopher Codrington and Henry Drax. The vast majority of planters in those days rejected the notion of educating the Blacks on the simple ground that literate slaves and ex-slaves did not generally make good manual labourers. They viewed all non-white peoples merely as a source of labour, specifically created by God to be hewers of wood and drawers of water. As was then the case throughout Europe, there was an uncomfortable feeling that even elementary training tended to make the lower classes dissatisfied and rebellious. It is also important to note that, while the benefactors had made their private fortunes through the toil and energy of Blacks, the free schools were not intended for that segment of the society. The education of Blacks and Coloureds was left entirely to the charity and private enterprise of missionaries and abolitionists. Moreover, nobody then thought it proper to educate the girls of either race. The whole idea behind the establishment of schools in the seventeenth and eighteenth centuries was based on the deliberate aim to strengthen the hegemony of white males.

There has been so much controversy over Combermere's origins that it is necessary to say here that a copy of Drax's will, dated 30 June 1682, is still extant in the Department of Archives in Barbados and makes it plain that he did provide for a free central school.[2] The will reads, in part:

> *Herein I give and devise for the erecting and enduring a Free school or College in Bridgetown, in the island of Barbados, to endure and continue for ever, to be paid by my Executors in England, three years after my decease, £2,000 . . . to the extent and purpose aforesaid.*

When his executors failed to carry out Drax's wishes promptly enough, the members of the St Michael's vestry petitioned the governor of Barbados in 1692 to force them to erect the school for which Drax had provided. The governor found it necessary to replace the original executors with an entirely new slate of trustees, composed of Hon Francis Bond, Benjamin Bullard, Hon John Farmer, Hon John Gibbs, Hon George Lillington, George Peers, Hon Richard Salter, Sir Timothy Thornhill and Hon Thomas Walrond. It was this group which became, in effect, the first governing body of the Free School.[3]

The new trustees proceeded to purchase, on 1 December 1692, seven acres of land for £140 from Hon William Howe, a judge and a member of the Legislative Council. H.G. Hutchinson, a local historian who taught for twenty years (1916-36) at Combermere School, was convinced that the governor and the members of the St Michael's vestry would not have deposed the old executors (who included such important planters as John Carrington, Christopher Codrington, Richard Guy, John Hothersall and Samuel Newton), and encouraged their successors to build a school on so much land, simply to leave it empty. He therefore concluded that he could "safely claim" that Combermere is unique among all colonial schools in having been born during the Stuart period.[4] Plans of the actual site are still visible among the *Recopied Deeds*, showing that the school was eventually built near the swamp close to the banks of the Indian River.[5]

It was there, on Constitution Hill, where the modern Queen's College for a long time and until very recently stood, that the free school for poor Whites was first situated. It was variously known as the Drax Parish School, the Colonial Charity School, the Parochial Charity School, the Free School, the Boys' Central School, and (much later) Combermere School. The Combermerians occupied those quarters until the 1940s when the school was relocated at Weymouth, off Roebuck Street. That the school was already in operation by the mid-1690s is clear from the records which show that it was used as a temporary prison for some French soldiers captured by the British in August 1696.[6] Vestry minutes also indicate that the Free School persisted throughout the eighteenth century.

One such item, dated 17 March 1717, is most revealing. It "ordered that the present Churchwarden pay unto Mr Dryher the Latin schoolmaster the sum of £10, as a present for his encouragement in erecting a school in this parish". The Drax Parish School was the only such institution that this note could then possibly have been referring to, since the Harrison Free School, which subsequently became Harrison College, was not founded until the 1730s.[7]

Very little, however, has been discovered about the school's early life. It is known that teaching began there in 1695 under Mr Allen, an Englishman, who was replaced in December the same year by Rev. James Hull whom the St Michael's vestry appointed "Lecturer of the Parish School". It catered for many years to a handful of pupils, taught by a single master, as was the custom in English primary schools in those days. Edward Harris and John Odell were among the earlier teachers, while George Clarke, Samuel Gallop and George Gill also taught there towards the end of the eighteenth century. By the 1790s, the school-leaving age was set at fourteen, and two masters were appointed by the St Michael's vestry. Two known headmasters during this period were John Hartley Phillips and a certain Mr Wiltshire.[8]

The Boys' Central School, 1819–79

This parish school was ultimately replaced by the Boys' Central School when a more elaborate building was erected on the same site with the help of funds provided by the Barbados Society for Promoting Christian Knowledge (BSPCK). It seems that a sequence of natural disasters, including the hurricane of 1780, had gradually left the original building, by the second decade of the nineteenth century, in a sad state of disrepair. Almost miraculously, the BSPCK had managed to collect over £5,000 from a fund-raising drive to build a school in the island's capital city to cater to pupils from all the parishes and to provide education for poor white and middle-class mulatto boys. The cornerstone of the new school was laid on 4 June 1819 by the Governor of Barbados, Sir Stapleton Cotton, the first Lord Combermere. He was himself the patron of the Barbados branch of the SPCK and wished to establish, as he put it, "a more

Lord Combermere, after whom the School was named

efficient, moral and religious system than the one now in practice". The Central School, built at a cost of £2,630, was one of the largest in the Caribbean at that time. It was placed under the immediate jurisdiction of a school board consisting mainly of the governors and directors of the BSPCK.[9]

The eclipse of the Parish School by the Central marked a turning point in the history of Barbadian education. Its success was due not only to the profound interest of a colonial governor but to the remarkable zeal of an Anglican leader who put considerable store on education. Unlike the local planters, who thought it potentially dangerous to educate the slaves, who outnumbered the owners by a substantial margin, Lord Combermere and Bishop William Hart Coleridge felt that the society as a whole could profit enormously from the spread of literacy and that the slaves could be made into more efficient workers as well as better Christians by being taught to read and write. Coleridge was especially interested in providing the Blacks with religious instruction. As progressive as he was in the context of his time, even he did not think it appropriate to educate the Blacks "beyond their station".[10] Hitherto, education in Barbados had been dominated by a few isolated benefactors, such as Sir John Gay Alleyne, Rowland Bulkeley, Christopher Codrington, Henry Drax and Captain Francis Williams, who left large sums of money for the purpose of building schools.[11] Now, the Anglican church and the colonial legislature became more directly involved in this activity, and elementary schools began to spring up steadily in every parish thereafter. By an Act of 1822, the Barbadian legislature put £800 annually at the disposal of the Central School which it placed under the general supervision of a governing body consisting of five senior members of the Council, one senior representative of each parish, all the Church of England clergymen in Barbados, all the subscribers of £20 (or £5 annually) and the Bishop of the diocese who was to serve as its president.[12]

This Education Act of 18 January 1822 actually put the colony in advance of the metropolis, since the British parliament did not make its first annual grant towards the promotion of elementary education until 1833, when £20,000 was earmarked for that purpose. Barbados, in fact, has traditionally remained ahead of Great Britain in matters of this kind. While the Barbadian benefactors recognized the urgent need to educate the children of poor white families, the voluntary associations in Britain had considerable difficulty persuading the establishment that a national system of education was necessary. It was not, therefore, before 1891 that a system of free elementary education was provided by the British government, and as late as 1902 A.J. Balfour, the prime minister, could justly complain that the education system in Great Britain was inferior to its European and U.S. counterparts. Even as late as 1914, secondary education still remained far beyond the reach of working-class families in that country.[13] In the aftermath of the 1816 slave rebellion, however, Lord Combermere was forced to respond to the varying demands of the imperial government, reactionary planters, liberal Coloureds and disgruntled Blacks. He took the view that a repressive programme would not have been appropriate.

When the Central School was opened in 1819, twenty-six children between the ages of eight and fourteen were admitted free. Two came from each of the eleven parishes, two from the United Lodge of the Masonic Body, and two from the English Charitable Society. They were to be educated, clothed, and boarded at the expense of the school trustees, while others could be admitted either as day pupils or as boarders upon such terms as individual vestries found agreeable. The twenty-six scholars were bound to the churchwardens for five years and were to be apprenticed to some trade for a further five years. The penalty for violating the bond was set at £25.[14]

In 1826, the parish of St Michael thought it necessary to build a girls' school in the vicinity at a cost of £1,893, for the express purpose of training the daughters of poor Whites. Again, the wardens were showing more progressive thinking than their counterparts in Britain. It is true that they were mainly concerned with the question of white female illiteracy, but the fact is that in the metropolis at this time, only a small minority of cultural leaders had yet accepted the principle that girls ought to be formally trained. The Girls' Central School evolved into Queen's College and eventually inherited the whole site on Constitution Hill when the boys departed in December 1943.[15] An Infants' Central School was also erected nearby so that there were three Central Schools in operation by

1833, catering to 134 boys and 92 girls, under the direction of Mr Rowe and Mrs M. Grayfoot, the latter of whom administered the infants and the girls. By this time, the original grant of £800 had to be shared by all the primary schools in St Michael, so that the three Central Schools between them had to operate on £512 16s. from the government, plus small voluntary contributions and interest from ancient trusts. The remaining £287 4s. presumably was earmarked for distribution among other elementary schools that were rapidly springing up in the parish.[16] Even so, the opportunities for manumitted young Blacks and Coloureds were so limited and government funding for them so minimal that the St Mary's School for Boys, established by the SPCK in 1818 to serve the needs of Blacks and Coloureds, continued for several years to struggle along on charitable donations from private individuals.[17]

The Boys' Central School appears to have prospered under the direction of John Brathwaite, the headmaster from 1838 to 1850. By 1846, the roll had reached eighty, consisting of fifty boarders and thirty day pupils.[18] By 1848, Brathwaite had persuaded the St Michael's vestry to contribute to the Central Schools, whose budget now included £512 from the government, £64 from the vestry, £25 from subscriptions and £144 from fees and interest.[19] Even in Brathwaite's last year, when the Boys' Central roll had fallen to seventy, including only thirteen boarders, the student body there was still larger than that of the Harrison Free School, which was catering in 1850 only to fifty-four boys, including twenty-three boarders. It is noteworthy that the school roll then contained the name of W. St Eval Atkinson, whose great grandsons all attended Combermere School almost a century later and two of whom, Denis and Eric, distinguished themselves by playing cricket for the West Indies.[20] The Atkinsons' attachment to Combermere over such a long period is unique in that they represented one of the few well-to-do white families in Barbados who preferred to send their sons to this institution long after the government had declared Harrison College and the Lodge School the only two first-grade secondary schools (for boys) in the island. These first-grade schools were intended for children of the expatriate and upper classes. They were different from the second-grade schools, in terms of the curriculum which was geared to university entrance and preparation for the professions, the quality of their staff which was predominately expatriate university graduates and their fees which were generally beyond the reach of the lower classes. The less generously funded second-grade schools catered to the poorer Whites and those Blacks who could afford secondary education for their children.

The Boys' Central School taught purely elementary subjects, stressing arithmetic, English and religious instruction until, in 1850, the school board imported two educators from England, Thomas Salkeld and R.P. Elliott, to run it. They materially changed the character of the Boys' Central School by making it much more than just an adjunct to the apprenticeship system, which had come into effect after the emancipation of the slaves in 1834. They stressed agriculture, carpentry and history in addition to the traditional three Rs and hoped to use the institution for producing more qualified teachers to staff the expanding elementary schools throughout the island. They appeared ready to model the Boys' Central on the pattern of the emerging grammar schools in Britain. Hence the building of a middle school, attached to the Boys' Central in 1854, for the provision of secondary education for the children of middle-class Whites. For some years, this appendix was known as the Central Middle School.[21]

In 1851, the roll of the Central Schools rose to 239, of whom 182 were boys, while the attendance at the Harrison Free School fell to 43. Salkeld had made an immediate impact, even though he was offered an annual salary of only £126 after Brathwaite had been paid £128 yearly during the 1840s.[22] The St Michael's vestry was so impressed with his work that it increased its annual grant to the Central Schools to £137 10s.[23] Unfortunately, however, Salkeld died of yellow fever that same year.[24]

On 1 December 1851 R.P. Elliott succeeded Salkeld as headmaster of the Boys' Central School, in which capacity he served until February 1859. Acting also as the first inspector of schools in Barbados, Elliott tried valiantly to continue Salkeld's work. But the steady increase of primary schools in the island eventually forced him to resign the headship of the Boys' Central when the duties of chief inspector became too onerous.[25]

While Brathwaite and Elliott had brought considerable stability to the Boys' Central School from 1838 to 1859, their immediate successors did not last long. Rev. Robert Ellis gave way within a year to Rev. S.F. Branch who also departed very shortly. J.P. Cawthorne then served as headmaster from 1860 to 1865, when G.F. Laurie was appointed by the board of directors, who now included the governor of Barbados, Robert Mundy; Hon Grant E. Thomas, president of the council; Hon Charles Packer, Speaker of the House of Assembly; Hon John Sealy, the attorney-general; Rev. Thomas Clarke; and Rev. H.H. Parry. Laurie remained headmaster until March 1869 when he became perhaps the most celebrated casualty in the history of Barbadian cricket. While playing the game, he suffered a serious injury from which he never recovered. J.A. Greenidge acted in his stead for a few months before giving way to Rev. Henry W. Moore in May. When Laurie died in October 1869, Moore succeeded to the headship.[26]

Effects of the Michinson Commission

Moore was the last headmaster of the Boys' Central School. He was still in office when the governor of Barbados, Rawson W. Rawson, appointed the famous commission, under Bishop John Michinson, to investigate all aspects of education in the colony. The commission interviewed Moore on 15 April 1874 and left an appendix on that conversation which throws some useful light now on the Boys' Central School in the early 1870s. Moore revealed that his total annual salary was £200 plus about £30 from capitation fees. Boarders were then required to pay £10 per annum and day boys were charged one shilling per week, payable in advance, for tuition. Total fees received from students in 1873 amounted to £33 15s. In that year, there were sixty-eight boys on the register, including twelve foundation boarders, twenty-eight free, and twenty-eight paying day pupils. While the admission age was flexible, the school leaving age was fixed at sixteen, except for pupil teachers who stayed on for some years more or less in the role of apprentices. Moore testified that most of the students from the Boys' Central went off to become clerks and bookkeepers. Only two of them, so far as he knew, had become teachers. He concluded that the majority avoided teaching for the simple reason that commerce and industry were far more lucrative fields. He also observed that most of the free scholars in recent years had been black.[27] After emancipation, it had apparently become increasingly difficult to exclude black children from the parish schools, which had originally been intended purely for the training of poor white children. Black families clearly understood even then that education was the only escape from poverty and the tedium of farm labour. While emancipation had provided them with personal freedom, it had done too little to improve their social and economic status.

The Michinson Commission reported promptly and fully to the governor in 1875. Its Report is one of the most significant documents in the history of Barbadian education. It emerged with a variety of far-reaching recommendations which became the cornerstone of education policy in Barbados for generations, and clearly inspired the all-important Education Acts of 1878 and 1890 which were not really superseded until the 1980s. The Michinson Commission recommended, *inter alia*, the expansion of elementary education at public expense, more provision for teacher training at all levels, better salaries for Barbadian teachers, more stress on the education of girls, and a total upgrading of secondary education in the island. Not enough attention had been paid to primary and elementary education of black children and there was a tragic shortage of teachers, schools and equipment. But by far the most gaping hole in the Barbadian system, so far as the Commission could judge, was the singular lack of institutions for the training of middle-class children. Apart from Harrison College and the Lodge School, it could point only to the small seminary in St Andrew with about twelve boys being taught by the curate of St Simon's Chapel, a tiny foundation school in St Lucy, and a slightly more successful "Pilgrim's Place" in Christ Church. These schools were left entirely to "private adventure", while a few clergymen also supplemented their income by offering private tuition. The whole system of secondary education in Barbados, in short, was much too haphazard.[28]

The commissioners concluded that there were too few opportunities for secondary education in Barbados. In keeping with the English experience, they naturally suggested a two-tiered system meant to provide an élitist education for the upper classes and a more utilitarian curriculum for the others. They were, in fact, thinking of reproducing a replica or two of the celebrated public schools as well as a number of the so-called grammar schools that were then emerging in Victorian Britain. The public schools were intended to cater to the wealthiest segments of the society and their fees were set in such a way as to deter the multitude. Hence the introduction of the notion of first-grade and second-grade secondary schools in Barbados. Accordingly the commissioners stressed the necessity of establishing more efficient second-grade schools to cater to pupils between the ages of nine and sixteen. They felt that a good second-grade secondary education should include arithmetic, English, scripture, geometry, elementary mathematics, Latin, perhaps some French, and a science subject. Taste could be cultivated by offering such optional subjects as art and music. The commissioners also felt that more opportunities for further study should be made available to brighter and wealthier students between the ages of sixteen and twenty. They therefore recommended a first-grade system which taught Greek, advanced Latin and higher mathematics, in addition to all second-grade subjects. As a result of these recommendations, Harrison College, the Lodge School and Queen's College (for girls) emerged in the early 1880s as first-grade secondary schools to be more fully subsidized by the government of Barbados thereafter. It is noteworthy, in this connection, that Barbados had again taken the lead over Great Britain which did not become heavily involved in providing for secondary education until 1902.[29]

It would be wrong, however, to assume that the Barbadian cultural and political leaders were behaving in an altruistic manner. The whole machinery of Barbadian politics was then still dominated by a small white plantocracy which controlled every aspect of the island's existence. With the steady collapse of the sugar cane industry in the West Indies, partly because of bad management and fierce competition from sugar beet producers elsewhere, Barbadian planters, who had previously sent their sons to be educated "properly" in British public schools, now hoped to have this quality of education provided for them at home, largely at public expense.

They therefore created an educational system which allowed them to send their children to Harrison College, the Lodge School and Queen's College, which they proceeded to fund much more generously than all of the other academic institutions in the colony. They also instituted more liberal Island and Barbados Scholarships with the view of procuring university training for some of their own offspring, at no cost to themselves.

It was the discussion of secondary education that drew the attention of the Michinson Commission to the Boys' Central which was then trapped in no man's land somewhere between the first-grade schools and the dozens of primary schools which dotted the landscape. The commission argued that the Boys' Central was ideally situated to be converted into a government aided secondary school and suggested that "the large grant from the legislature now expended on this institution, without commensurate advantages derived from it, may more wisely be distributed in grants in aid to the series of second grade schools above indicated".[30]

Thus it was that the Boys' Central came to be promoted in 1879 to a full-fledged secondary school while ironically losing a considerable portion of its former government subsidy. By the Central Schools Act of 1859, the government had again set aside £800 for these institutions, whose budget in 1873 exceeded £1,127.[31] But in 1879, to find the necessary money to support other secondary schools, the government had to revise its original grants quite drastically. The Boys' Central was detached from the Girls' and Infants' schools on Constitution Hill and was also officially renamed Combermere School as a tribute to the governor who had shown such a keen interest in its earlier fortunes.[32]

By the late 1870s, then, the government had established a clear distinction between first-grade and second-grade secondary schools in Barbados. This was in keeping with contemporary developments in other territories in the British West Indies. But the Barbadian experience differed from that of other islands in that the class distinctions inherent in the experiment were destined to survive much longer there than anywhere else. The annual tuition fees for Harrison College, the Lodge School and Queen's College were set at £15 (i.e. beyond the capacity of lower middle-income families), while those for the second-grade schools were fixed at £5. The first-grade schools were deliberately intended to cater to the wealthier classes and consistently received preferential treatment from successive governments thereafter, until the invidious distinctions between first-grade and second-grade secondary education in Barbados were abolished altogether by Errol Barrow's Democratic Labour Party (DLP) government in the early 1960s. In fact, the student population of the Barbadian first-grade schools remained largely White until the 1940s and very few Blacks were appointed to their teaching staff before the 1950s. The creation of Queen's College as a first-grade secondary school was a significant development in the education of Barbadian girls and was perhaps intended to parallel the establishment at this time of similar institutions in Britain.

But the Education Act of 1878 had also established Combermere, thanks to its strategic location, as the leading second-grade secondary school in the island. Although its annual grant was reduced to £200, it began with distinct advantages over the Alleyne, Coleridge and Parry Schools which were also elevated to second-grade status.[33] Indeed, those "rural" schools each received only £100 annually from the state and were always much less generously funded than Combermere. They were each still receiving £100 in 1899 when the Combermere grant had increased to £300.[34] Combermere at once attracted even more students from the outlying parishes while Alleyne, Coleridge and Parry, geographically isolated as they were, tended for many years to remain somewhat parochial. By the turn of the century, when the average attendance at Combermere School stood at 120, the numbers for Alleyne, Coleridge and Parry were no better than eleven, thirty, and twenty respectively.[35]

The Role of Rev. Thomas Lyall Speed

The first headmaster of the newly reconstituted Combermere School was Rev. Thomas Lyall Speed, a former curate of St David's and St Lawrence. He had been educated at the Lodge School and had served as third master there under Rev. Charles Clarke in the late 1860s and very briefly afterwards at Harrison College under Horace Deighton, one of the most famous headmasters in West Indian history.[36] Well-liked by the boys, with whom he often played cricket, Speed earned the respect also of the parents and the public. Under him, Combermere steadily grew in numbers and stature. Its roll increased from 70 in the 1870s to 127 in the early 1890s.[37] To accommodate increasing numbers after 1879, new buildings had to be erected at a cost of £350, but the school still lacked adequate playing fields. Speed, who had himself represented Barbados in the first intercolonial cricket match ever played in the Caribbean, was particularly concerned over the absence of a cricket ground.[38] He recommended (vainly) in 1894 that perhaps some land in Belleville might be leased as a cricket field for the school.[39]

In Moore's last days as headmaster of the Boys' Central School, he had been assisted only by three pupil teachers, but Speed was allowed one assistant master when he was appointed in 1879. His salary, too, was superior to Moore's. He was offered £100 per annum plus capitation fees of £3 for each pupil up to 80, £2 for every boy between 80 and 120, and £1 for each student after that. Thus, in 1883, when the average attendance was 79, his salary came to £337. By 1883, he had also been allowed to appoint two other masters. The Combermere staff in that year thus included J.A. Harbin, C.H. Giles and W.H.B. Massiah, each receiving £80, £70, and £65 respectively.[40] By 1889, when the Combermere roll reached 87, and Harbin and Massiah had left, the staff now included P.R. Farnum and J.G. Wilson, while Giles, first appointed in January 1882, had now become first assistant master (the equivalent of a modern deputy principal) at £80 per year. The part-time music instructor, at £20 annually, was M.E. Doorly.[41] Cyril Dear was appointed in July 1890 and C. Foderingham was added to the staff in 1892, when there were 119 students in regular attendance. These two junior masters were offered £50 each per annum. When J.E. Chaderton replaced Farnum in May 1894, all the senior assistants (with the exception of Giles) received a promotion and an increase in salary. In January that year, E. Bedford also replaced Doorly as the music teacher.[42]

During the 1890s, capitation fees were also paid to the senior masters as a bonus. Thus, in 1894, Speed received an extra £312, Giles £58, Wilson £29, and Dear £19. One year later, with a slight increase in attendance, these bonuses came respectively to £321, £60, £30, and £30, while Chaderton and Foderingham received only their basic annual salaries of £50 each.[43]

By the mid-1890s, there were six forms at Combermere School, including the preparatory for younger pupils. The staff had stabilized itself at six, including the headmaster, plus a part-time musician. The curriculum was amended, in 1891, to include arithmetic, scripture, mathematics, English grammar, composition and literature, elementary Latin, French, geography, history, drawing, vocal music and drill. To counter the increase in student numbers and the expansion of the curriculum, the government grant of £200 per year had been supplemented by a small subsidy of £53 from the St Michael's vestry, but this was still insufficient to meet the school's needs. This was reflected in the salaries paid to Speed's staff. In 1894, when Deighton at Harrison College was being paid £1,000 in basic salary and bonuses, Speed himself was receiving only £412 pounds, including capitation fees, and his assistants' annual salaries then ranged only from £50 to £138. It is therefore not surprising that he found it very difficult to attract qualified teachers.[44]

Speed's staffing problems sprang from an acute shortage of funds. Monies available to the government in those days were seriously and consistently limited by the plantocracy's dogged refusal to impose just and adequate taxes upon itself. The island's revenues were derived mainly from indirect taxation which fell most heavily and unfairly upon the lowest classes. Since the planters at the same time insisted on paying very low wages to their agricultural labourers, the latter (who then formed the bulk of the purchasing public) were always unable to contribute significantly to the public purse.[45] These basic difficulties were destined to persevere until the government came manfully to grips with income and land taxation during the last days of colonialism. The Combermere budget, as late as 1892, still stood at a mere £382 plus fees, or approximately £1,000.[46] The school's governing body was, therefore, much restricted in its options. Nor can it be said that the Barbadian legislature, given its avowed commitment to the principle of minimal direct taxation, was unreasonably parsimonious. The last three decades of the nineteenth century were generally years of severe economic hardship for all sugar-producing communities and Barbados was particularly hard hit. At a time of serious economic stress, the island's government was spending more than £15,000 each year on its primary and secondary schools.[47] Indeed, during a particularly bad year, 1895, when the colony's revenues had fallen (in one year) from £160,624 to £146,315, the government still spent more than £20,000 on all branches of education (including grants to the public library, the Department of Science and Agriculture, and the government industrial schools). To commit more than 13.7% of its total revenues to education was most unusual in those days and it is not surprising that the government should have set up an Education Commission, under Bishop Bree in 1894, to consider how the education budget might significantly be reduced.[48]

This exercise in the interest of strict economy produced no tangible result, especially since most of the people interviewed, including Speed himself, emphasized the need for additional rather than reduced spending. The vast bulk of the witnesses appearing before the Bree Commission called unequivocally for higher salaries for teachers, and this opinion was most vigorously expressed by Rev. N.H. Greenidge, the Parry School's headmaster.[49] The government was unable to do more than offer Combermere School an additional £100 annually in 1896, but even this was offset by the simultaneous withdrawal of the small contribution previously made by the St Michael's vestry. Thus, the Combermere revenues that year amounted only to £943.[50]

This helps perhaps to explain why the school's governing body was so anxious to alter the headmaster's contract when Speed died in 1896. In his stead, A.F. Hernaman, M.A. was appointed at an annual salary of £250 plus considerably reduced capitation fees. The old system of bonuses was overhauled to the disadvantage of the senior masters. No capitation fees were offered for the first fifty students; only £1 was given for each student between fifty and a hundred; and 10 shillings for every pupil in excess of a hundred. Thus with an official attendance of 105 in 1896, Hernaman's gross income was just slightly more than £300.[51]

Financial problems notwithstanding, Speed administered Combermere with conspicuous success during his seventeen years as headmaster. It was he who patiently laid the foundations upon which the reputation of the school could be built by his immediate successors. He made Combermere one of the finest academic institutions in the Caribbean during the late Victorian age. It became famous as a commercial school as distinct from the first-grade secondary schools which were focusing narrowly on the classics. By 1896, Combermere had become known as one of the best training grounds for future businessmen in the West Indies. It was no longer catering simply to children of lower middle-income Whites but had already begun to provide middle-class black children with secondary education. It was, in fact, the first Barbadian school to do so, although the Whites in the colony had long been outnumbered by more than ten to one.[52] Prolonged economic depression also persuaded some of the planters and the merchants to send their sons to Combermere, so that while the numbers at the first-grade schools often dwindled during the age of Speed, Combermere's enrolments did the opposite. This was especially the case from 1879 to 1882 when the situation at the Lodge had become so critical that the school actually closed its doors for several months.

Combermere School and the Wider Society in the 19th Century

The growth of Combermere School during the nineteenth century was in keeping with other developments in Barbadian life. It first of all reflected the steady emergence of a coloured bourgeoisie, led by such individuals as Anthony Barclay, Lincoln Bourne, Samuel Francis Collymore, Thomas Cummins, Thomas Harris, Joseph Kennedy, James A. Lynch, Charles Phipps, Samuel Jackman Prescod and Sir Conrad Reeves, then by far the most persuasive advocates of Barbadian civil rights. Operating in the stifling atmosphere of overt racism accompanied by the worst forms of snobbery, this class had to fight an uphill battle to persuade the plantocratic élite to pass the few remedial measures that were grudgingly enacted in the post-emancipation period. Some of their efforts would most surely have come to naught had they not occasionally won the moral support of the Colonial Office. The British society was itself a conservative one, but its leaders had long seen the need for pacifying the multitude and had passed an almost incredible sequence of social and economic reforms dating back to the 1830s.[53] In sharp contrast, the Barbadian élite, living always in mortal fear of Black *revanche*, failed to follow the metropolitan example and often refused to heed the moderate advice offered by the metropolis.[54]

The steady growth of Combermere also reflected the society's increasing concern with the question of literacy, especially after the cessation in 1846 of the imperial grant, first made in 1835, to the West Indian colonies for the express purpose of educating the Blacks in the immediate post-emancipation era.[55] The Barbadian legislature, cajoled and otherwise influenced by such liberals as Samuel Jackman Prescod and such educators as Richard Rawle, played a prominent role, too, passing several vital education acts which committed the government to increasingly generous provisions for primary and then for secondary education.[56] The Act of 24 October 1850, for instance, created the office of Inspector of Schools and established the Education Committee, which it empowered to spend £3,000 over the next two years. As this subsidy was perpetuated, the ultimate effect was the doubling of the annual grant of £750, provided by the Act of 21 July 1846, for primary institutions apart from the Central Schools already funded by the Act of 1822.[57] This statute was superseded by that of 21 December 1858 which placed all public schools under the Education Committee, and offered financial assistance to any school with more than fifty students. It also raised the education grant to £5,000 for two years and promised to pay £300 to any school catering to middle-class children.[58]

All of these earlier bills were dwarfed and indeed repealed by the Education Act of 9 December 1878 which established the Education Board and a better-paid inspectorate to implement the suggestions of the Michinson Commission. It was so all-embracing as to establish the very foundations of modern education in Barbados. It was the first statute to provide generously on an annual basis for all levels of training. It also did much to formalize the granting of Island and Barbados Scholarships.[59] It paved the way for the Education Acts of 1890 and 1897 which began the process of centralization which was destined, in the long run, to bring the administration of all Barbadian schools under the immediate control of the ministry of education.

Rev. Lyall Speed, however, did not have to contend with some of the restrictions which have, in some ways, reduced the effectiveness of Barbadian headmasters and headmistresses in our own time. He was still left by the Scheme of Government of 1890 with very wide powers with respect to the choice of books, methods of teaching, arrangement of classes and school hours, and in general the whole internal organisation of the school. He acted, of course, under the general supervision of the governing body that was responsible to the Education Board, but he was allowed considerable latitude in areas of staffing and discipline. He, in effect, administered Combermere School and was expected to do so.[60] This remained the Barbadian tradition until very recently.

There can be no doubt that Speed performed his duties very capably indeed. He left a profound impression on all of his contemporaries. His commitment to drawing, vocal music, drill and cricket allowed those disciplines to take such deep root that none of his successors could easily have eradicated them. He was acclaimed an excellent teacher at a time when headmasters were required to teach more than to administer. He was also an effective administrator during a crucial period of Combermere's transition. It is a real tribute to his spadework that Combermere never relinquished its position as the leading second-grade secondary school in Barbados. Speed's position in the history of the school is also recognized by the fact that one of the Houses (Set D) is named after him. An enlarged photograph of him, presented to Combermere in 1928 by a grateful alumnus, H.C. King, still hangs conspicuously in the school hall today.[61]

Speed brought Combermere into line with the grammar schools that were then sprouting up all over Britain and, like his counterparts at Harrison College and the Lodge School, tried to copy as many of the British models as he could. He thus played a notable role in the anglicization of Barbadian education at the end of the Victorian age. It may well be true that some of the British disciplines and techniques were inappropriate in a Caribbean setting, but they were

Rev. T. Lyall Speed, Headmaster 1879-96

the only ones which Speed and his Barbadian contemporaries knew. The process of anglicization, in any case, had begun before the age of Speed. He was simply continuing in the tradition of such famous educators as Coleridge, Deighton, Elliott, Michinson and Salkeld.

In one significant respect, however, Speed's institution differed from its British counterparts. Whereas the latter focused narrowly on the classics and humanities, then considered the prerequisites for gentility, Combermere broadened its curriculum to cater to the needs of the mercantile elements within the society. Combermere was deliberately intended, after all, to train its boys for lower middle-income positions, while the vast majority of secondary schools throughout Britain and the empire were geared towards supplying the needs of the aristocracy and the upper middle-classes. This was the case, for example, with Harrison College and the Lodge, designated first-grade by the Education Act of 1878, as well as the few grammar schools that began to appear in other colonies within the Caribbean area. In Speed's time, several West Indian parents seeking a practical secondary education for their sons found Combermere a very attractive option. Thus it was, for instance, that George Learmond, son of well-to-do Guyanese parents of Scottish descent, could spend much of his youth in Barbados as a Combermerian during the 1890s. In 1900, he became, in effect, the first old Combermerian to gain selection on a West Indian touring cricket team.[62]

This tradition of training its pupils for making practical contributions to the wider community was never really lost. For most of the twentieth century, Combermere continued to provide Barbados with a disproportionate bulk of its accountants, clerks, managers, civil servants, and elementary school teachers. The example set by Speed and Learmond on the cricket field was also followed by several generations of Combermerians.

Chapter Two

THE ROLE OF GEORGE BISHOP RICHARDSON BURTON

When Rev. Speed died in 1896 he was succeeded as headmaster of Combermere School by A.F. Hernaman who left shortly thereafter to assume the headship of the Lodge School.[1] It was in 1897 that the governing body decided to appoint G.B.R. Burton, who had applied unsuccessfully for the headship in the previous year.[2] This proved to be an excellent choice. Burton remained at the helm of Combermere for more than a quarter of a century and left an indelible imprint on the school.

Burton was born in Barbados in 1859. His father, George James Burton, was an Englishman who had become manager of Hope Plantation and had married Sarah Jane Bell, who was descended from a distinguished family of planters, including Sir Philip Bell, one of the earliest English settlers in Barbados. Burton's parents thus belonged to that small White minority which then dominated Barbadian life. The young Burton attended the Boys' Central School during the headship of Rev. Moore before proceeding to Harrison College in the 1870s. There he came under the influence of Horace Deighton, who had arrived from England in 1872 with the firm determination to mould Harrison College into a replica of a Victorian public school. Stressing the classics, cricket and corporal punishment, Deighton ultimately made Harrison College one of the greatest secondary schools throughout the British empire.[3] Burton won an Island Scholarship in 1877 and graduated with a classics

G.B.R. Burton, Headmaster 1897–1925

degree from Codrington College in 1880. He then taught briefly at Parry School before becoming headmaster of Coleridge School in 1882, when he was only twenty-three years old. He is reputed to have raised the standard of education there almost to the first-grade level and it was his enviable reputation as a headmaster at that school which preceded him to Combermere in 1897.[4]

Burton went to Combermere at a time when the economic slump, resulting from the worldwide collapse of the sugar cane market, was seriously affecting enrolments at both secondary and primary schools in Barbados. The Combermere student body, which had reached 127 in the early 1890s, had declined to 102 by the time of Hernaman's departure. It is much to Burton's credit that he improved the image of the school and made it so popular that by 1921 there were 259 pupils on its register.[5] These included a number of children of merchants and smaller planters, who, in happier times, would no doubt have attended one of the first-grade schools. Combermere simply could not accommodate so many bodies and in the early 1920s Burton had to place a limit on admissions. By the time of his retirement in 1925 the numbers had therefore been reduced to a more comfortable 200.[6]

At the Coleridge and Parry Schools Burton had demonstrated a remarkable gift as a teacher. He had been a hard-working tutor, insisting on giving individual attention to the slower students. He went to Combermere with the same attitude and thus aroused the displeasure of some of the older teachers there. The conflict between the new headmaster and his assistants was freely discussed in letters to the editor of the *Barbados Advocate*, the leading daily newspaper in the island, whose files now provide invaluable insights into Burton's character and methods. He thought it his duty, as a public servant, to respond patiently to a number of questions raised by a 'Taxpayer' in December 1897.[7] He told the Barbadian people that, as headmaster of Combermere School, he regarded the fifth form, the most senior grade, as his own responsibility. He taught all the subjects in that form without confining himself exclusively to it. He visited every other form at least once a week, as he considered himself a general supervisor of the work being done by his staff. He felt very strongly that teachers should correct all exercises before the next lesson so that the slower pupils would be able to keep pace with the more gifted. He insisted on this practice even if it meant that his assistants had to remain at school each day for an extra hour or more. As for corporal punishment, which was then so much in vogue in British and colonial schools, he felt that it should be discreetly used. In his judgement, indiscriminate flogging did more harm than good.[8]

In the crucial early days of Burton's headship, when the staff was unhappy about having to work overtime both in and outside the classroom for very little reward, 'Pin' and 'Medicus' thought it necessary to write strong letters to the *Advocate* in his support. 'Medicus' was especially confident that Burton would perform at Combermere the same miracles that he had wrought at Coleridge. He considered the new headmaster a conscientious teacher who would win a number of Island Scholarships for his school, if only his pupils were allowed to study Greek.[9] At this time, however, in accordance with the Education Act of 1890, only the first-grade secondary schools were allowed to do so.

Positive statements of this kind were frequently repeated in the pages of the local press, with the *Advocate* once observing that Burton's boys were showing a marked mental as well as physical improvement since his staff evinced "as much interest in the boys in the playground as in the school room".[10] In 1900, Oliver DeC. Emtage, the Lodge School headmaster, and Arthur Somers Cox, the famous scholar/athlete who later became headmaster of Harrison College, who were then serving as Combermere's external examiners, reported favourably on the school's academic work and suggested that an institution doing so much and doing it so well deserved at least one more assistant master and a good deal more financial aid than the £300 which the government was then allocating to it each year. The editor of the *Barbados Advocate* agreed that the results reflected much credit on the school's headmaster and his staff.[11] That daily newspaper was also able to remark in 1901 that "Combermere School has made a distinct place for itself owing to the very practical bent of its teaching".[12]

This observation sprang from Burton's determination to make Combermere a supplement, rather than a competitor, to the first-grade schools. He stressed commercial subjects and deliberately prepared students for service in the community rather than for passing examinations in the humanities and the classics. Hence Combermere, under Burton (and as it had begun to do under Speed), made a name for itself as the ideal institution for training pupils for a mercantile career. The school offered instruction in English composition, précis writing, shorthand, typewriting, bookkeeping, commercial arithmetic, French and Spanish. When Emtage and Somers Cox presented another favourable report on Combermere in 1901, the *Advocate* once again praised the drive and energy of Burton and his assistants.[13] Later, in 1918, Burton took the revolutionary step of creating a special commercial class with a separate form master. Students graduating from the third form could enter the commercial stream to prepare for certificates offered by the London Chamber of Commerce (LCC) or proceed to the fourth form to sit the Cambridge School Certificate examination in the traditional manner.[14]

Burton's miracles became so well known that Combermere's popularity and prestige reached greater heights than before. This is evidenced by the keen interest manifested by the social and cultural élite of Barbados in its annual Sports and Speech Days. At most of these functions, Burton took the opportunity to complain bitterly about the palpable inadequacy of funding, staffing, space and playgrounds.[15] In 1902 these complaints were discussed in the Barbadian House of Assembly.[16] Some members of the legislature, especially R.J. Clinkett, E.B. Skeete and J.O. Wright, deplored the sad state of affairs of the school. They emphasized the lack of space, books and equipment, the need for proper furniture, and the fact that the teachers were so poorly paid. Skeete thought it grossly unfair that the legislature should grant Harrison College £1,000 to support 132 students, and the Lodge School £500 to educate 46, while Combermere, with an average attendance in excess of 150, received only £300 per annum. The editor of the *Advocate* readily agreed that somehow the funds requested by Burton had to be found to repair the school buildings and to increase the salaries of the staff, since:

> *At the Combermere School, special efforts are put forth to enable boys to advance to first-grade schools or to at once endeavour to equip themselves for immediate employment. The success that has up to the present attended these efforts is very marked and calls for special consideration from the Education Board.*[17]

In the education debates of 1903, Aubrey Goodman, the solicitor-general, also made a strong plea for increasing Combermere's share of the annual grant for second-grade schools. He found it improper that the government should grant the other second-grade schools £100 each per year to train fewer than thirty pupils while restricting Combermere to an annual grant of £300. He called therefore for a graduated scale, in accordance with attendance. His proposal, however, was criticized (especially by H.W. Reece, the representative for St Lucy) on the ground that it could only be done at the expense of Alleyne, Coleridge and Parry. The House of Assembly could not support a measure which conceivably would have resulted in the collapse of the rural secondary schools, nor was the legislature in favour of treating the first-grade schools less preferentially than it had previously done. And no one, of course, considered the simple expedient of broadening the tax base to ensure that the plantocrats shouldered their fair share of the island's fiscal burden. The formal motion to increase the Combermere School grant was thus defeated by a margin of thirteen votes to seven. The motion to amalgamate the Coleridge and Parry schools also failed by an even more decisive margin of sixteen to four.[18]

Minor amendments to the Education Act of 1890 were the only tangible result of these parliamentary debates. In May 1903, new schemes of government were promulgated for the second-grade secondary schools in Barbados, now consisting of Alleyne, Coleridge, Combermere and Parry for boys, plus the Alexandra and Victoria Girls' schools. But the new regulations were not much different from the old. Combermere's revised Scheme of Government, for instance, merely acknowledged a *fait accompli* by bringing its curriculum officially into line with what Burton had already established on his own initiative. The governing body was now left with the authority to appoint the headmaster and to dismiss him on a term's notice (three months instead of six as before). The headmaster was to receive a fixed salary of £250 per year in addition to such capitation fees and bonuses as the governing body might determine for each pupil in excess of fifty. Boys were now to be eligible for admission up to seventeen years instead of fifteen as formerly. All prizes were thereafter to be determined by the headmaster rather than the governing body. And a further £75, earmarked for Victoria School, would be passed on to Combermere should the enrolment at that girls' school fall to less than eight. The few minor economies attempted by the new scheme of government produced only a minimal effect on Combermere's budget. The school's estimated revenues for 1903-04 still amounted only to £1,270, including government grants, tuition fees and ancient trusts.[19]

Rapid Expansion under Burton

By this time, Combermere's regular staff had increased to seven, in addition to three visiting masters teaching commercial subjects. Burton had persuaded E.B. Skeete, a Bridgetown accountant, to undertake the bookkeeping classes (which he successfully did for almost nineteen years); while Woodbine Forde, the leader writer for the *Barbados Agricultural Reporter* and a part-time teacher at Harrison College, was the visiting Spanish master; and A.B. Price, the House of Assembly's official reporter, taught shorthand on a part-time basis.[20] Still, despite all the difficulties facing the school with respect to attracting and retaining permanent teachers, or persuading the government to fund it adequately, Combermere's enrolment jumped to 184 by August 1903.[21] Thus, within six years of his appointment, Burton had seen the student body almost double itself. These statistics are more meaningful when placed alongside those of other secondary schools in Barbados. The Alexandra, Alleyne, Coleridge, Parry and Victoria schools then boasted average attendances of forty one, ten, twenty, twenty, and six respectively. Apart from Combermere, the largest then was Harrison College with 138 students in 1903, when the Queen's College roll stood at 117.[22] The student body at the Lodge School, on the other hand, numbered only fifty in 1903 and did not exceed 100 until 1926.[23]

Despite Combermere's spectacular expansion in Burton's early years, the Barbadian government could do little to accommodate the increasing numbers. The school's governing body, operating on a shoestring budget as it was, could do nothing. It was in vain that Burton kept on pleading for more generous funding. At the Speech

Day ceremony in 1909, he plaintively called for overdue repairs to old buildings, the immediate erection of new ones, and an increase of salary for his underpaid assistants. They were being blatantly overworked, saddled as they were with huge and cumbersome classes. Edward Laborde, one of the most promising of them, had recently left £90 at Combermere, as Burton lamented, to take £150 from the Lodge School where he was actually teaching fewer students.[24] His complaints fell to some degree on deaf ears but more particularly, on empty pockets. The fact is that Barbados was already spending huge sums on all levels of instruction and could not keep pace with the heavy demands being constantly made by a society which placed so much store on education. In 1903, for example, the colony's total education budget exceeded £21,000 at a time when its entire revenues amounted only to £185,353.[25]

Burton, however, was largely objecting to the inequitable manner in which the limited funds were being distributed. He could not but observe that the first-grade secondary schools, whatever the justice of their own complaints, were receiving preferential treatment. This was destined to remain a thorny issue mitigated only in some measure when the distinctions between first-grade and second-grade secondary schools were swept aside in the 1960s. The crux of the problem, of course, was the continuing reluctance of the plantocracy to establish an appropriate fiscal system that would permit those most capable of paying taxes to contribute their fair share to the public treasury. As late as 1913, it was still possible for an official at the Colonial Office to complain about the tragic fact that over 97% of the island's tax revenue was derived from customs and excise, while only minimal sums were being collected from landed estates and private incomes.[26]

Early in the twentieth century, the government of Barbados was subsidising more elementary schools per square mile than anywhere else in the world. In this small island of 166 square miles, there were 166 elementary schools in 1907; and still everywhere there was considerable pressure on space. While the colony lacked the resources to keep buildings in good repair and at the same time to provide secondary education for more than a few hundred students, class and race were undoubtedly important variables in the allocation of its limited funds.[27] Barbados would also have been able to do much better had the white élite adopted a more progressive approach to both the questions of taxing itself properly and providing the Blacks with quality education. There was still a general feeling among the upper classes that the whole society would suffer untold mischief should the Blacks be given an overdose of academic medication. Even the editor of the normally moderate *Barbados Agricultural Reporter* was able to state, towards the end of 1905, that while "some book-learning is of course essential", it would be a grave "mistake" to convey to the black child "the idea that such education as he acquires at school is calculated to make him eligible for the highest honours in life".[28]

The Education Commission set up by the Barbados government in 1907 under Bishop W.P. Swaby readily acknowledged the existing financial constraints. The commissioners did feel, however, that Combermere School was seriously underfunded. It contained too many unwieldy classes and too few masters. Since there were only as many masters as forms, there could be no effective division of groups for the purpose of specialization. The headmaster himself was required to do so much teaching that it was impossible for him to attend properly to his administrative and supervisory tasks.[29]

The exploitation of Combermere's teachers, whose annual salaries ranged from £75 to £145, was also deplored by the Swaby Commission. The inevitable result was that the Combermere staff remained extremely unstable. The low salaries could not attract the ablest teachers, so that young men, searching merely for a stop gap in their late teens, had to be recruited directly from school. This had obviously led to a loss of continuity in the school's work. The Commission concluded that the Barbadian government would never attract men with degrees to teach at the secondary level unless it were willing to pay higher salaries and revise the pension scheme to put teachers in line with the civil servants and to encourage transfers across imperial boundaries.[30]

The Swaby Commission found the Combermere classrooms too small and too few to accommodate the current number of pupils. The rooms were also so close together that one class had necessarily to interfere with its neighbours. The Commission accordingly

G.B.R. Burton, staff and student body in 1910, near the School on Constitution Hill

recommended the building of a spacious and proper school hall for assembly; six large classrooms, with twenty square feet each for twenty-five boys; two small classrooms for bookkeeping, shorthand and Spanish; a consulting room for the headmaster; a school library; a senior common room, equipped with a proper lavatory, for the masters; a new and more sanitary lavatory for the boys; a bicycle shed for the pupils; a small armoury for such equipment as cadet rifles; and a carriage house and stable for the headmaster. The commission felt that most of these problems could be solved by adding a third storey to the present building and increasing the supply of chairs and desks to enable better instruction in art, physics and mechanics which it wanted to add to the Combermere curriculum.

The commission estimated that these changes and additional furniture would cost the government £1,000. It also thought that the government should budget for an additional assistant master to ensure the proper teaching of so many students. The current establishment of one head, five assistants and three visitors was totally inadequate. In fact, the commissioners argued that it would be better and more economical to dispense altogether with the three part-timers and appoint a single master on a permanent basis to teach bookkeeping, shorthand and Spanish. They earnestly recommended an increase in salary for the headmaster and all of his staff. They would increase Burton's annual income to £400, including all allowances and capitation fees, his first assistant's to £180, and the remaining five salaries to £500 divided in such a way as the governing body thought fit. They would also discontinue the practice of paying capitation fees to assistants. The commission also suggested that the annual grant of £300 to the school's governing body be doubled to bring Combermere's income up to £1,480 per annum. This was but a small price to pay for "a school which is doing so important a work for the middle classes of Bridgetown and its neighbourhood".[31]

Effects of the Swaby Commission

The important Swaby Commission produced some immediate improvements to the school buildings and only minimal increases to the salaries paid to its teachers. Burton, for instance, received only £347 in 1911 and £351 in 1912.[32] But within a few years it seemed to have brought an end to the chaotic staffing situation of which it had complained. Certainly, during the first fifteen years of Burton's tenure, the Combermere staff was most unstable. The first assistant master, Giles, died in 1903 after serving the school for twenty-one years and was replaced by E.G. Bowen, a former Lodge School teacher with many years of experience and a degree from Codrington College; but he resigned in 1906.[33] The first three Spanish masters, in quick succession, were E. Cordle, R. Parravicino and Woodbine Forde. Alfred Price taught shorthand at the turn of the century but his services were terminated when that subject, for financial reasons, had to be undertaken by the regular staff. Cyril Dear, who was first appointed in July 1890, left eventually in 1906 with his salary still stagnant at £65 per year. A. Reece, who joined the staff in place of Chaderton in 1901, was replaced by L.E. Deane in the following year. By 1908, Deane had left. J.I.C. Howard, a Codrington College graduate, succeeded Foderingham during the first term, 1901-02, but departed in 1908. Laborde, who was appointed in January 1908, resigned in September the same year. H.D. Bayne, appointed in 1908, resigned in 1909. Charles Wilkinson Springer, one of the first black men to graduate from Codrington College with an M.A. degree in classics, acted for some time before being given a permanent post on 13 January 1908. He died at twenty-seven in October 1914, when his son Hugh (the late Sir Hugh, a former governor general of Barbados) was but an infant. He was replaced by Leo R. Hutchinson, fresh from the fifth form, but who went off to the battle front in September 1915. Hutchinson returned to the Combermere staff when the Great War ended but resigned in 1921. R.E. Batson, after a brief stint, resigned in 1912 and left for Scotland to study medicine. Hugh Arrindell, C.S. Batson, Rev. Caspar Downie, A.F. Mandeville, F.S. Walcott and Weatherhead, the drill instructor, all came and went with bewildering rapidity.[34]

It is really a credit to Burton's skill and patience that he succeeded in maintaining the highest standards in the midst of such chaos. It is also to his credit that he managed thereafter to attract a stable group of loyal assistants who were prepared to make substantial sacrifices to keep up the good work at Combermere notwithstanding the inadequacy of their monetary rewards. The Combermere staff, in fact, became almost completely static during the last decade of Burton's headship. It did so, notwithstanding the fact that its members were required to teach each day, without any off-periods at all, from 10 a.m. to 4 p.m. and beyond; to be totally responsible for all the subjects taught in their respective forms; and to take part in as many of the extracurricular activities as possible.[35] All of these teachers, the bulk of whom were white, would most certainly have been much better off had they sought employment in the business firms, or served as commission agents in Bridgetown. They could have done a great deal better in a financial sense, too, had they become assistant managers, accountants or foremen on some of the bigger plantations in the country. Some of their own classmates, such as T.O. Bryan, Cuthbert Lisle Gibbs, St Clair Hunte, Vernon Knight, Evan Lobo, R.B. McKenzie, Dudley Sarjeant, J.P. Taylor and Bruce Weatherhead, did remarkably well in the contemporary Barbadian business world.[36] A casual glance at the *Advocate Year Book and Who's*

Who 1951 is most revealing. The majority of commercial leaders listed there were the products of Burton's Combermere.

A Stable Staff at Last

A careful examination of Burton's later assistants speaks volumes for the magnetism of his own personality. John 'Gladio' Wilson, who had first been appointed in 1886, remained on the Combermere staff until his retirement at sixty-five in 1932. He had served as first assistant master for twenty-six years.[37] W.H. Carter, appointed in September 1908, did not leave until 1926 when he assumed the headship of Foundation Boys' School.[38] V.A. Southwell was appointed in September 1909. His association with Combermere was destined to last until 1944, even though he was considered a visiting master during the last twenty years (when he taught part-time also at Harrison College).[39] Frank Collymore's whole life revolved around the school which he first entered as a pupil in 1903. Fresh from the fifth form in 1909, he was invited by Burton to take up an acting position on the staff. This was converted into a permanent post in January 1910. Collymore taught at Combermere until 1963, despite his official retirement, at the age of sixty five, in 1958.[40] L.L. 'Goot' Webster, as Richard Batson's replacement, served the school from 1912 to 1950, leaving a notable impact on its athletics as well as on its teaching of geography.[41] H.G. Hutchinson, who ultimately came to grief when the preparatory form was abolished in 1936, had by that time been on the Combermere staff for twenty years.[42] B.F. Hall, appointed to a permanent position in 1916, after having acted in L.R. Hutchinson's place for one year, resigned in 1929 to become a priest.[43] V.B. Williams, affectionately known by several generations of schoolboys as the 'Bull', eventually retired more than forty years after his initial appointment on the Combermere staff in 1919.[44] And C.F.A. Corbin, universally remembered simply as 'Bing', gave the school unbroken service from September 1921 to January 1956.[45]

Burton had an incredibly stable staff with which to operate after 1914. He could therefore succeed in developing a certain *esprit de corps*, especially since he himself had taught the majority of his young appointees. Collymore, Corbin and Williams, for instance, were all Combermerians who joined the staff immediately after leaving the fifth form. They knew of Burton's emphasis on the personal touch in teaching and of his insistence that the teachers should play a prominent role in the extracurricular activities of the school. From the point of view of academic qualifications, they had been inadequately trained, as none of them had gone beyond the Cambridge School Certificate. On the other hand, Burton had carefully hand-picked and trained them in his own peculiar style for service to their alma mater. In his Speech Day address in 1914, Burton made much of the fact that six of his seven assistants were working extremely hard outside the classroom. He was not surprised, he said, because five of them had been his former students and therefore appreciated the value of extracurricular activity.[46]

Ironically, it was during the earlier period of instability that Burton had introduced the Cambridge School Certificate and also made Combermere the first school in Barbados to prepare students for the London Chamber of Commerce examinations. He clearly recognized the need for training in the field of business, while the first-grade schools were still concentrating on Greek, Latin and higher mathematics. As the *Advocate* often acknowledged, Combermere became a boon not only to Bridgetown and St Michael (the central parish in Barbados) but to the outlying parishes and the neighbouring Caribbean islands as well.[47] With its tuition fees permanently fixed at £5 per year, Combermere, under Burton, consolidated its position as the major secondary school catering to the needs of the lower middle classes. It became the haven for emerging Blacks and did more to staff the industrial and commercial houses in Bridgetown than any other academic institution. This was freely admitted by the editor of the *Barbados Agricultural Reporter* who, early in 1910, argued very strongly in favour of more generous funding for Burton's school.[48]

Burton himself had been a classical scholar in his youth and continued to take particular interest in the teaching of Latin at his school, but he insisted on teaching all the subjects in the fifth form. He took great pride in coaching all of the fifth formers for their

Cambridge School Certificates. However one of his former pupils, Frank Gibbons, who finished first in the junior first-grade scholarship examination[49] in 1920 and moved on to Harrison College, remained convinced that this was the one glaring defect in the Burton system.[50] After 1920, as Burton grew older and the fifth formers became more numerous, he was unable (in Gibbons's opinion) to provide the necessary magic. The Combermere examination results, especially at the senior School Certificate level, declined noticeably in Burton's last years.

Examination Results, 1913–26

A careful study of these results during the last twelve years of Burton's stewardship lends considerable support to Gibbons's claims. The 1913 results were very good indeed. Nine of twelve Combermere candidates passed the Cambridge School Certificate, with H.A.M. Beckles (at the age of fifteen) placing second among all the Barbadian candidates and achieving four distinctions. Five of six students also passed the junior School Certificate. Even some of the failures did quite well in the commercial subjects that year.[51] The juniors were less successful in 1914, but all five seniors passed.[52] In 1916, seven of nine seniors won certificates while eight of nine juniors passed, including Hilton Vaughan who gained a distinction in Spanish.[53] In 1917, six of seven Combermerians passed their School Certificate and the seventh was most unlucky in that he had not passed in a foreign language. He had actually achieved a distinction in arithmetic, placing second among all Barbadian students in that subject. Vaughan came second with a distinction in English and C.F.A. Corbin placed tenth overall. Seven juniors passed among the nine entered.[54]

The turning point came in 1918, when the school signally failed to adjust to the new Cambridge regulations which required certificate holders to be proficient in a minimum of five subjects, including English language, Latin, mathematics and one science subject. Even the strongest candidate failed that year, as he could not pass one of the compulsory subjects, despite his eleven credits.[55] This fact was bitterly bemoaned by the headmaster who argued that the new Cambridge rules were much too rigid.[56] All nine juniors passed in 1919, but Burton again had cause to regret the severity of the new regulations which denied A.A. Hinds a senior School Certificate after he had passed in ten subjects but had failed only in geography (then classified as a science option). Three of the five seniors were successful that year.[57] In his Speech Day address on 4 April 1921, Burton summarily dismissed the examination results as being more unsatisfactory than usual.[58] Three of five seniors, and nine of thirteen juniors, passed in 1922.[59] The results from 1923 to 1926 were uniformly bad. The nadir was reached when all three Combermere candidates failed in 1926. The fact that only three students were considered fit enough to attempt the examination that year was itself cause for some unease.[60] Burton tried to combat the new Cambridge rules by introducing a sixth form in 1922 to give his seniors an additional year to prepare for the School Certificate, but that manoeuvre produced no immediate effect.[61] It is noteworthy, however, that even in the bleakest year, 1926, the junior certificate results could still be described as "exceptionally good".[62] The fact is that the juniors performed consistently better than the seniors who continued to fail miserably until the Burton system of personal tutoring at the sixth form level was abandoned by his immediate successor.

It was not only the senior Cambridge candidates whom Burton personally coached. He also gave private tuition, in many instances free of charge on Saturday mornings, to the brighter youngsters whom he prepared carefully for the first-grade scholarship examinations to Harrison College. In this way, he thus deprived Combermere, year after year, of its most promising scholars by helping them to win places in the first-grade school. Many young Combermerians in Burton's time thus went off to Harrison College where they ultimately won the prestigious Barbados and Island scholarships. A number of distinguished Old Combermerians, in other words, also became distinguished Old Harrisonians. C.V.H. Archer, H.A.M. Beckles, J.W.B. Chenery, F.L. Gibbons, E.M. Sealy, E.G. Stroud and L.A. Walcott are but a few such examples.[63]

Non-Academic Pursuits at Burton's Combermere

If the Burton stamp on the Combermere curriculum is noticeable to this day, so too is his mark on the extracurricular life of the school. It was he who did most to create the Combermere School Cadet Company in 1904 and to keep it alive in the difficult period immediately afterwards. Burton had always been a keen advocate of physical education and as early as 1899 had made physical drill a compulsory part of the curriculum.[64] He now encouraged such young teachers as Henry Bayne and Francis Walcott to establish the cadet corps on a permanent basis. Captain R. Radcliffe Hall, then an officer in the Volunteer Force in Barbados, gave invaluable help with the drilling and administration of the Combermere company in its infancy. It soon joined with Harrison College and the Lodge School to form the Cadet Battalion of the Volunteer Forces in 1909. Under the capable guidance of Hugh Arrindell and William Carter, two young assistant masters, the Combermere School Cadet Company prospered, reaching a roll of sixty-two in 1913.[65] Arrindell resigned in 1916 to enter a commercial career,[66] but Burton always succeeded in persuading younger teachers to participate actively in Combermere's physical drills. Thus, for instance, he cajoled Collymore and Williams to serve as cadet officers in the early 1920s.[67] He also encouraged student participation in the cadets by introducing the practice of awarding an annual prize to the most efficient boy in the company.[68]

It was under Burton, too, that the Combermere Scout Troop, the first in Barbados, was founded in 1912. Its first leader was Arrindell who managed immediately to attract as many as sixty-four members; but he was himself too busy with the cadets and had to give way to Springer, another young colleague. One of the most energetic of Burton's assistants, Springer was the first editor of the *Combermere School Magazine*. He took up scouting with remarkable enthusiasm and was the initial driving force behind the school's troop. Under his leadership, Combermere was presented with the much-coveted King's Flag on 7 March 1914 for being selected the most deserving troop throughout the British empire.[69] After Springer's premature death from typhoid fever that same year, the Scout Troop was kept alive by the untiring zeal and devotion of Carter and Southwell. Burton also remained very interested in scouting and was himself the honorary secretary of the Scouts' Association of Barbados during the 1920s.[70]

Another Burton tradition which has survived is the house and prefect system which he introduced "to promote a healthy rivalry amongst the boys of the school so as to make them keener at books and games".[71] This idea was deliberately copied from the English public school system of houses and house masters. Burton divided the school into three sets, A, B and C, and placed each set under the general supervision of an assistant master. The first set masters in 1912 were Collymore, Southwell and Webster. Each set had two prefects (chosen from among the senior boys) to assist with the matter of conduct and discipline. Each boy had to be attached to a set and could achieve set points by taking part in a wide range of activities, as set points were awarded for virtually everything. For example, a first-class honours result in the Cambridge examinations meant one hundred set points; coming first in the form during the term brought twenty-five, joining the scouts or cadets carried fifteen set points, and ten were awarded for each player who made the school's cricket or football team.[72] To encourage greater involvement, two masters and two more prefects were attached to each set in 1914.[73]

In January 1924, Burton revised the system, limiting each set to one master and one prefect while giving more authority to eight form monitors.[74] When the assistant masters expressed some dissatisfaction with the amended house system, Burton again revised it, more drastically on this occasion, in September 1924. He now divided the school into two sets, A and B, under Collymore and Southwell. But the sets included only the upper forms as Burton aimed to give the senior boys more responsibility by supplying them with junior fags to protect. Each set was left with one master and two prefects, while a new school committee was established. The school committee included the headmaster, the assistant masters, the prefects, the school captain, the games captains, and the senior scout and cadet from each set. The system of form monitors also survived, as did the idea of maintaining student representation on the Combermere school magazine committee.[75] The fagging experiment, however, was a total failure and was promptly abandoned when Burton retired.

The house and prefect system, in part, was the product of Burton's commitment to the cult of athleticism. He had not himself been an athlete in his youth, but he recognized the value of games and remained convinced that they contained some magical power capable of strengthening the moral fibre of his pupils. In this respect he was a staunch disciple of Horace Deighton who did perhaps more than any other apostle to spread the gospel of muscular Christianity throughout the Caribbean.[76] Like Deighton, Burton sincerely believed that "brains are of no use without a sound body".[77] He thought that the Great War had made this even more obvious. Hence his eloquent plea, in 1919, for playing fields spacious enough to train pupils properly in physical education, should the British empire ever need protection again.[78] Even before the Anglo-Boer War, Burton had introduced the annual Sports Day in April 1898 although Combermere had only minimal space for athletics on Constitution Hill. This severe handicap eventually compelled the school to hold its annual Sports Day at Kensington Oval and then, after 1924, at Queen's Park.[79] The assistant masters served as track officials during these functions and perhaps the keenest among them was 'Goot' Webster who remained the official starter for many years. One of the brightest of the early athletic stars at Combermere was John Smith who later became the headmaster of Parry School before teaching at his alma mater during the 1950s.[80]

Burton's interest in athletics led him to give moral support also to such emerging sports as cricket and soccer. The school had no space for a cricket field, but in 1903 it was still admitted into the second division of the Barbados competition by the Cup Committee. Under Burton, the Combermerians played cricket with commendable zeal and the school produced such fine stars as L.S. Birkett, B.I. Gilkes, Herman Griffith, R.F. Griffiths, E.L.G. Hoad, L.R. Hutchinson, J.M. Kidney, C.C. Rogers and Herbert Rogers, all of whom represented Barbados in intercolonial tournaments.[81] Burton also encouraged his staff to take an active interest in the game which ultimately emerged in a most extraordinary manner as the island's peculiar national symbol.[82] Among Burton's staff, the most devoted athletes were Collymore and Williams who formed the backbone of the school's cricket and football teams for an aggregate of almost sixty years.

Burton also tried valiantly to bequeath to Combermerians the tradition of a school magazine which he himself did so much to create and to keep alive during the last twelve years of his stewardship. Religiously each term, from June 1913 to December 1925, the *Combermere School Magazine* appeared. Its first editor, Charles Springer, was succeeded in 1914 by Victor Southwell, who held the post until 1924. In 1922 he took the very progressive step of creating an editorial committee on which he invited the senior monitors and prefects to serve.[83] When Southwell resigned his full-t ime appointment in order to serve both Combermere and Harrison College in the capacity of a visiting master, the task of editing the magazine fell to Collymore.[84] Almost symbolically, there was no issue during the term immediately following Burton's retirement.

The magazine reappeared in September 1926, entitled the *Combermerian*, and was an annual publication for about twenty years thereafter. During the 1940s, when publishing costs became prohibitive, it was discontinued. All efforts to revive it have so far failed, and only one or two intermittent annuals have appeared since 1950. It is from the volumes of the magazine that a good deal of the school's early history can now be gleaned. Burton himself contributed several articles to the initial issues. But even though he traced the roots of the school back to the immortal will of Colonel Henry Drax, who died in 1683, he somewhat illogically celebrated Combermere's centenary in an impressive ceremony on 4 June 1919.[85]

A vital portion of the Burton legacy is the present Combermere School Old Scholars' Association (CSOSA) which had its roots in the Combermere Mutual Improvement Association founded in 1914 to promote the mental, physical and moral development of Combermerians past and present. Its numbers grew rapidly to 165 by 1922 and it prospered for many years.[86] It was out of this organization that the idea of a Combermere School Old Boys' Association (CSOBA) eventually sprang.

It was the phenomenal success of Old Combermerians that added much to the positive image of the school during the period of Burton's headship. Year after year, Speech Day produced glowing tributes from a long succession of governors of Barbados who consistently drew attention to the marvellous manner in which Combermere Old Boys were flourishing in so many parts of the world. Some of the alumni, too, attracted considerable praise by departing for the battle front after 1914 as soon as they could. Some earned military distinctions while others sacrificed their lives for the greater glory of the British empire. Burton himself was so proud of the school's contribution to the imperial war effort that he initiated a fund-raising campaign in 1922 to erect a plaque as a memorial to Old Combermerians killed during the war. The fund eventually stalled at $186 after two years, but an impressive War Memorial ceremony was held at the school on 4 June 1924 when a tablet was unveiled and the fourteen martyrs commemorated. Sixty-eight known Old Boys had participated in the Great War, twenty-one had been wounded or gassed, ten had died in action, and four had died from wounds. On the brighter side, two old Combermerians had won the Military Cross, three had been awarded a Military Medal, and two had received Distinguished Conduct Medals. For a colonial school of its size, Combermere had certainly made a noteworthy contribution. Of this, Burton remained inordinately proud to the end of his days.[87]

Burton Remembered

'Old Pa B.', as he was affectionately known by the boys, eventually retired from the headship of Combermere in December 1925 at the age of sixty-six. During his twenty-eight years as headmaster, some 1,700 boys, by his own calculation, had passed through Combermere.[88] It is almost impossible, in trying to evaluate his role, to exaggerate Burton's contribution to the school's evolution. He built most effectively on the foundations left by Speed and made Combermere one of the most respected secondary schools throughout the Caribbean. It became famous for its teaching skills although the majority of its teachers had not themselves been formally trained. They had the incalculable advantage of having been coached by Burton himself. He always stressed that a teacher's job did not end at 4 p.m., and he compelled his assistants to work in many instances for unconscionably long hours. He never ceased to regard the duller pupils as capable of salvation and forever insisted that extra attention be focused on them.

It is not surprising, then, that Combermere established a lofty reputation under Burton as one of the best schools in the British empire. Notwithstanding his great leadership qualities and administrative talents, it was really as a teacher that he himself excelled. As his contemporaries freely acknowledged, he inherently possessed quite extraordinary skills in this area. He therefore came to serve as a source of inspiration to a variety of colleagues who instinctively recognized that they were not as gifted as was Burton himself. He also served as a source of inspiration to hundreds of students who consciously tried to pattern themselves after him. And yet, as he so often declared, he never aimed primarily at producing good results in formal examinations. He claimed that too many boys came to Combermere too late and too ill-prepared to be coached for certificates. His avowed objective was to prepare his wards in a very practical way for useful service within the wider community. Above all, he wished to produce constructive and law-abiding citizens rather than brilliant scholars.[89] This helps, in large measure, to explain why so many Old Combermerians who had achieved so little by way of academic distinction while at school were yet able to leave their mark in so many diverse fields afterwards.

As a Barbadian educator, Burton's influence was enormous. He was among the first to advocate a timely withdrawal from the kinds of curricula that were still in vogue at the public and grammar schools in Edwardian Britain. He began with the premise that all education had practical utility since it could help to cultivate the mind. He felt, for instance, that Greek and Latin had "sterling value as instruments of mental training". But he argued, nevertheless, that the continuing emphasis on the classics was overdone. Schools should retain classical studies, but should devote fewer periods to them and pay more attention to such disciplines as art, botany and music. In Burton's view, the Germans had demonstrated the tremendous value of modern languages, physical geography and the sciences. These were obvious lessons from which the British empire could well profit. The Great War had also shown how vital were cadets and scouts. Burton issued a clear warning, however, against rushing into extremes and churning out "mere materialists" as the Germans had unfortunately chosen to do.[90] His own handling of the Combermere curriculum from the beginning clearly put him in the forefront of Barbadian reformers.

There can be no question about Burton's abilities as an administrator. He ran his school in very much the same way as a Victorian captain would have run his ship. While he assumed total command, he was never regarded as despotic. In matters of discipline and supervision, he was very strict but fair and gentlemanly. He personally supervised every iota of Combermere School life and yet he managed to keep his assistant masters continually involved in the various activities of the school. His one great miscalculation was in not recognizing when the time had come for him to relinquish some of the responsibility for teaching all subjects at the senior level. Even so, considering the staff with whom he had to deal, that decision is understandable. Most of his assistant masters had themselves been educated only up to the level of the senior School Certificate.

A measure of Burton's overall influence is the distinguished list of persons who received their formal training at Combermere School in his time. Among a host of others, this honour roll includes such famous names as C.V.H. Archer, Professor Cyril Atkins, Rev. Reginald Barrow (father of the late Errol Barrow, prime minister, and Dame Nita, present governor general of Barbados), H.A.M. Beckles, Frank Bishop, Chris Brathwaite, T.O. Bryan, W.H. Carter, Major A. DeV. Chase, J.W.B. Chenery, Dr Belfield Clarke, Frank Collymore, Wynter Crawford, Professor J. Sydney Dash, George Ferguson, Dr H.I. Hamlet, E. St A. Holder, Dr Reginald Hunte, Dr E.D. Laborde, Canon A.F. Mandeville, Fred Miller, Sir Frank Newsam, Dudley Sarjeant, Captain Rueben Sealy, E.M. Shilstone, Hilton Vaughan, Bruce Weatherhead and Captain Herbert Williams.[91]

G.B.R. Burton's success as a headmaster was based as much on the singular warmth of his personality as on the profundity of his scholarship and the strength of his administrative skills. Although his manner and appearance suggested a certain Victorian primness and austerity, he always proved, beneath the surface, to be a disarmingly warm and witty individual—as his senior pupils invariably discovered.[92] He was thus able to establish a fine rapport with students as well as colleagues. The high esteem in which Burton was universally held is clear from the extant records. All his surviving students still speak of him with a reverence amounting to filial piety. This was true even of such a crusty old war horse as Frank Gibbons, to whom the authors had a chance to speak in 1986.[93] Burton was an immensely popular headmaster as is evidenced by the emotional ceremony which took place at Combermere shortly after his retirement. A large number of Old Combermerians gathered on that occasion to show their appreciation of Burton's work and to present him with a silver tray and a cheque. Chris Brathwaite, Leo Hutchinson and Jack Kidney spoke with much feeling about what 'Old Pa B.' had meant to them.[94] It is very seldom indeed that a headmaster succeeds in capturing the hearts of his pupils so completely. Burton richly deserved the warm tribute paid him by the Combermere Alumni Association, U.S.A., some sixteen years after his death when they presented the school with a beautiful commemorative plaque. In a simple but touching ceremony on 21 July 1949, his daughter Norah, then headmistress of St Michael's Girls' School (now the St Michael School), unveiled the Burton plaque at Weymouth.[95] It now fittingly adorns the assembly hall at Waterford. Several features of present-day Combermere life are legacies of the Burton era. He left the school so well established that within ten years of his retirement its enrolment would exceed 300, despite the economic miseries which then plagued the whole Caribbean region.[96] Without the remarkable work of George Bishop Richardson Burton, this would hardly have been possible.

It is to Burton's credit, too, that he was able to steer his school so successfully through a difficult age of social transition. During the first quarter of the twentieth century, the coloured and black bourgeoisie in Barbados continued its steady growth. This was due, in part, to the infusion of "Panama money" into the local economy. It is estimated that as much as £546,000 was remitted to Barbados from that country between 1906 and 1920. Barbadian emigrants, who had found regular employment when the Panama canal was being built, not only bought small plots of land in their native colony but tried desperately to ensure that their children received some form of secondary education.[97] Hence the continuing demand for space at Combermere, which had largely been white in Burton's early days. The school became increasingly mixed. Racial tensions still existed in the wider society, but it was Burton's school which demonstrated, perhaps more graphically than any other Barbadian institution at that time, that desegregation could produce positive results. It is true that Burton did not appoint Blacks as teachers, apart from the outstanding and exceptional Springer (who would surely have become a staff member of one of the first-grade schools had he been white); but such observant and critical contemporaries as Chris Brathwaite, Frank Gibbons and Chamberlain Hope (all Old Combermerians who were black) did not attach much importance to this curious fact. To their dying days, they remained, in fact, among his staunchest supporters and were prepared to vouch for his impartiality and intelligence.

Chapter Three

COMBERMERE SCHOOL 1926-1946: TWENTY YEARS OF RAPID GROWTH

G.B.R. Burton's successor as headmaster of Combermere School in January 1926 was the legendary scholar/athlete, G.B.Y. 'Gussie' Cox, who had been one of the greatest all-rounders in West Indian cricket at the turn of the century. He had the unique distinction of playing cricket for his native Barbados and for Antigua, where he had briefly taught in the 1890s. He enjoyed the even greater distinction of having scored the first century for Barbados in intercolonial cricket at Kensington Oval. He had accomplished that feat at British Guiana's expense in September 1897.[1] Cox had continued to play both cricket and soccer for many years while teaching at Harrison College.

The Influence of G.B.Y. Cox

Gussie Cox thus went to Combermere with an enormous reputation as a sportsman. He was one of the most popular idols in Barbados at that time. He was also, of course, much more than that. He had taught at Harrison College for thirty-one years and had built up a name for himself as a good, if not exceptional, classics teacher. The son of a dry goods store manager, Cox was born on 30 May 1870. He entered Harrison College as a pupil in 1881 and won an Island Scholarship in 1888. He graduated from Codrington College with a good classics degree in 1891. He taught at Coke College in Antigua from 1891 to 1893 and returned to Barbados to take up a permanent position at Harrison College in January 1894. Cox was thus, like Burton before him, a Horace Deighton product who had, not surprisingly, cultivated a healthy respect for athletic competition, classical learning, and strict discipline. His background and training had been very similar to those of his predecessors and he therefore brought to Combermere many of the same attitudes that had been assumed by Burton and Speed before him.[2]

Cox inherited a remarkably stable and energetic staff. His first assistant master was Wilson, who had already served the school for forty years. The others, in order of seniority, were Collymore, Carter, Webster, Hutchinson, Williams, Corbin and Hall. The visiting master was Southwell who had been associated with the school for seventeen years. When Carter left to take up his new appointment as headmaster of Foundation School at the end of the first term, O.A. 'Graffie' Pilgrim was appointed in his stead on 1 May 1926. Apart from Pilgrim, who had excelled at athletics, cricket, and mathematics at the Lodge School, the others were mainly Old Combermerians whom Burton had personally handpicked for service to their alma mater.

During the eight years that Cox spent at Combermere he was required to make only minimal changes to this staff. Only two permanent appointments, Frank 'Froggie' Gibbons to replace Hall and H.F. Bert Alkins in place of Wilson, and four acting appointments were made.[3] The routine established by Burton was very well understood by the staff who already were experienced teachers by the time of Cox's arrival. There was really little need for him to change the system, and given the well-known traditions of the school and the attitudes of the older staff members it would in any case have been very difficult for him to do so. Such changes as were made were contingent on the departure of existing staff.[4] After Carter's resignation, Corbin administered the cadets quite capably throughout the Cox years, and Williams, ably assisted by Pilgrim, made the Combermere School Scout Troop one of the most efficient in the island. Collymore and Hutchinson kept the *Combermerian* alive. Webster continued to take charge of athletics, and the school was run more or less in the same manner in which it had operated in the last twelve years of Burton's headship. Among the teachers, Collymore had clearly emerged as the most reliable lieutenant and had long been serving as Burton's right-hand man, rather than the temperamental Wilson, who was apparently more interested in his part-time career as a land surveyor. It was 'Colly', by all accounts, who really served as the catalyst and ensured the smooth transition from the Burton to the Cox regime.[5]

This is not to say that Cox sat still and allowed Burton's troops to fight his wars. He agreed, it is true, with much that Burton had done, but he also brought a fresh perspective to his task. He was by no means as gifted a teacher as Burton had been, but he was, in the opinion of many, a more alert administrator.[6] He at once abolished the two-house system, with which Burton had been experimenting since 1924, and restored the more rational three that had been there in the first place.[7] He also brought more sanity to the sixth form by utilizing his personnel more effectively than Burton had done. The latter had persisted in doing all the senior Cambridge tutoring himself. Cox altered that policy immediately. He naturally taught Latin to the older boys himself, but he also encouraged the rest of the staff to participate more actively in fifth and sixth form teaching. Thus Gibbons and Pilgrim were assigned to teach mathematics in the upper forms; Collymore taught French and English to the junior and senior Cambridge School Certificate candidates; and Webster took charge of the geography classes in the upper school.[8]

This system of specialization seemed to produce a marked effect on Combermere's examination results. Whereas the senior School Certificate results had been most unsatisfactory from 1918 to 1927, they now showed some improvement. In 1927, all three Combermere candidates failed the senior Cambridge School Certificate; but in 1928, four of five seniors passed and all eight juniors were successful.[9] The LCC results were also very creditable throughout Cox's reign. He appeared more willing to screen the senior candidates very carefully, entering only those who were most likely to succeed. Hence only three Combermerians were allowed to write the senior Cambridge School Certificate in 1929. On the other hand, sixteen were entered for the Junior School Certificate that year and twelve of them passed. Four of seven passed the senior examination in 1930, while seven of nine juniors were successful.[10] This system of rigid screening at the sixth form level and the tendency of some boys to leave school after achieving the junior School Certificate combine to make analysis of examination results quite difficult for that period. Even so, it is clear that Combermere's academic accomplishments under Cox were superior to those of Burton's later years. Of course it must be noted that the staff had by now also become more accustomed to the stricter Cambridge regulations.

Cox, then, did not alter the curriculum or introduce new classes or bring in a whole slate of new men. He steered the Combermere ship in roughly the same direction in which Burton had steered it. He tried for a while to encourage technical and manual skills by hiring a visiting expert, C. Devonish, to conduct carpentry classes on Saturday mornings. This apparently failed and he had to content himself with allowing a regular member of staff (Gibbons) to take over the woodwork classes in 1930. Gibbons was an expert joiner and carpenter and sometimes made props to help Collymore stage plays.[11] In effect, he did for some years under Cox precisely what Carter had for a long time done under Burton.[12] The carpentry classes, however, were never very popular.

But the Cox regime differed from Burton's in one fundamental particular. It had to cope, especially in the 1930s, with a revolutionary pressure on space, as more and more Barbadians, especially those in the lower middle-income range, sought secondary education for their children. Curiously, the Combermere enrolment, after a dramatic explosion from 146 in 1903 to 259 in 1921, had steadily declined throughout the early 1920s.[13] By 1926, the numbers had fallen to approximately 180.[14] The nadir was reached during the 1926-27 academic year when only 158 pupils were in attendance. This prompted an anxious letter from H.B.G. Austin, the chairman of the school's governing body, who wondered whether Cox could explain this serious decline. He was most concerned over the damaging effects of the sinking enrolments on the school's finances. The loss of thirty students, in concrete terms, meant the loss of £150 in annual fees—a significant portion of the school's budget at that time. In 1925-26, for instance, the total Combermere budget came to £2,538, of which tuition fees accounted for £1,168, almost half.[15]

Prophetically, Cox assured Austin that the problem was temporary. It was due, he thought, more to the general economic climate in Barbados than to any loss of stature on Combermere's part. A fair number of Combermerians, he added, had been tempted by the lure of Armstrong Scholarships[16] and had left for Harrison College.[17] Cox's analysis was definitely incorrect. Traditionally, enrolments at Harrison College, the Lodge School and Queen's College had provided a fair gauge of the economic climate. In times of economic hardship, in fact, some of the less prosperous planters and merchants in the island sent their sons to Combermere, rather than to the first-grade schools. As the education of girls was still not yet regarded as a priority in the way that it is now, the enrolment at Queen's College could also be expected to reflect the economic circumstances of the time. But average attendance at Queen's College had actually risen between 1920 and 1927 from 131 to 139. The roll at Harrison College had fallen only very slightly from 209 in 1920 to 191 in 1927. That is to say, Harrison College was affected only slightly, if at all, by the economic climate and did not, on the other hand, appear to have profited much from the Combermere exodus. Some of the other schools might have done so, as enrolments over the same span had actually increased at the Lodge School (from 99 to 112), at the Alleyne School (from 16 to 19), at Coleridge (from 25 to 49), and at Foundation (from 48 to 63).[18] Almost miraculously, however, it was at this point that the Combermere numbers began to increase again. By 1930, there were 200 names on the Combermere register. By 1931-32, the average attendance rose to more than 220 per term, and at the time of Cox's last Speech Day, in 1934, he was able to report that the number of pupils had risen to 240.[19]

An Age of Spectacular Expansion

The spectacular increase in Combermere's student body throughout the 1930s forced the government at long last to respond to the urgent appeals for additional accommodation, which the school had been making since the turn of the century. The report of the Swaby Commission had brought some temporary relief after 1910, but by Cox's last days it had become impossible to teach more than 220 boys in the available space on Constitution Hill. The school's governing body, operating then, as it had always done, on a notoriously inadequate budget, recommended a series of stopgap arrangements, beginning with major renovations to the old buildings in the summer of 1928. A.B. Franklin, a local contractor, was then employed to provide improved lavatory facilities and some additional space at a cost of £2,000. But still the acute shortage of space remained.[20]

It is true that Cox failed to persuade the governing body to provide the additional accommodation that had become so necessary after 1928, but it cannot be said that Combermere suffered from his headship. If anything, the school profited from one distinct advantage under Cox in that he and Austin, who had often played cricket together (for Wanderers and Barbados), retained a healthy respect for each other. Their friendship was an asset to Combermere at a time of considerable austerity. In 1929-30, for example, Barbados was already devoting almost £74,000 to education at all levels when the total revenues of the island stood only at £453,802.[21] With the government persisting with its outmoded fiscal policies, which left the propertied classes almost exempt from direct taxation, there simply was not enough money to spend on secondary education in those days and all governing bodies had necessarily to behave in a frugal manner. Austin, who was also the chairman of the Harrison College governing body, always seemed more sympathetic to Cox's requests than to those of Harold Haskell, the Harrison College headmaster, with whom he had much less in common.[22] Cox was at least able to squeeze a raise in salary from £450 to £500 per annum from a parsimonious governing body in September 1932.[23]

This final concession was made to Cox because the governing body feared a hiatus in the school's leadership if both he and Wilson, his first assistant master, left at roughly the same time. Cox had given notice of his intention to retire in 1932 just one term after Wilson's departure.[24] The governing body encouraged him to stay on until 1934 because they did not feel that the school could cope with the simultaneous retirement of its two most experienced staff members. Collymore was promoted to the rank of first assistant master in 1932, having been strongly supported by a petition from his colleagues who feared that an outsider might be invited to take Wilson's place.[25] In addition, a contingent of four staff members paid a visit to Austin's home at Enmore to plead Collymore's case. Austin gave them little encouragement at that interview, though he supported their position very strongly in subsequent governing body meetings.[26]

The Combermere staff petition, which Cox presented to the governing body in November 1931, is a most interesting document. It began with the fervent prayer that no outsider be brought in to have precedence over them. That would clearly be inimical to the school's best interests. It then emphasized the long-standing Combermere tradition that the resignation of one member automatically led to the promotion of the survivors in order of seniority. That, it declared, had in fact been made most explicit by Burton when he had appointed the majority of them. It concluded with the hope that:

> *you will consider our position carefully, since, inasmuch as we have devoted ourselves to the interests and welfare of the Combermere School, and have obtained results which compare favourably with those obtained by first-grade schools, it would be disheartening to feel that our labours were unappreciated.*[27]

In a carefully worded reply, the governing body acceded to the petition but made it quite clear that they had done so in the best interests of the school while still reserving the right, in principle, to choose an outsider if they felt that Combermere could profit from such an appointment. All the staff members thus gained promotions and slight salary increases in 1932.[28] Collymore's appointment as first assistant master in 1932 ensured a distinct measure of continuity. He had already rendered yeoman service to Combermere since 1909 and was destined to continue serving the school as teacher and member of the Combemere governing body until 1973.

In evaluating Cox's role, it seems clear that he consolidated Burton's work. He continued the Cambridge and LCC examinations in which Combermere achieved satisfactory results, especially in the commercial subjects. Not surprisingly, the school also excelled in the field of sports. Combermere was promoted to the first division in the cricket competition after having finished as the runner-up to the second division champions in 1928-29.[29] It then produced the mighty J.E. Derek Sealy, who rose to great heights as a cricketer while still in his teens. He was the outstanding Combermerian star during the period of Cox's tenure. Sealy was much encouraged by such staff members as Collymore, Williams and Pilgrim. Pilgrim had himself played cricket with much distinction for Spartan and Barbados. During this period, Combermere also produced such fine cricketers as 'Mannie' Martindale and 'Foffie' Williams, who eventually represented Barbados and the West Indies. Combermere's status and image simply had to profit from the basic fact that, from 1926 to 1934, it was led by one of the most celebrated idols in the island. Gussie Cox is still fondly remembered more than thirty years after his death (in 1958) as one of the legendary heroes of Barbados.

The Advent of Rev. Armstrong

In September 1934, Cox was succeeded as Combermere's headmaster by Rev. Arthur Evelyn Armstrong, popularly known as 'Buff'. Born in April 1881, Armstrong had been educated at Combermere School under Speed, and at Harrison College under Deighton. He won an Island Scholarship in 1899 and graduated from Codrington College in 1905 with degrees in classics and Divinity. After his ordination in 1906, he served for ten years as vicar of St Margaret's before moving on to St David's in a similar capacity from 1916 to 1921. He then administered the Armstrong Private School between 1921 and 1934 while also substituting occasionally at Harrison College when regular staff members were ill.[30]

Armstrong thus brought to Combermere considerable experience as a priest and a teacher. Like Cox, he was a scholar/athlete, having played cricket for many years for Pickwick and St Ann's and served as an umpire in intercolonial cricket matches. He was also very keen on scouting and community service. In his later years he became Island

Rev. A.E. Armstrong, Headmaster 1934–46

Cartoon of the staff sketched by Frank Collymore in 1935

Scout Commissioner as well as president of the YMCA. His background was thus so similar to that of Cox that he was hardly likely to introduce any drastic changes in the Combermere curriculum or administration. He was, in any case, too amiable and easygoing (some have actually said indolent) to exert himself in any extraordinary manner.[31]

Armstrong inherited virtually the same staff that Burton had left in 1926. The majority of his assistant masters were experienced teachers who had become accustomed to a certain system and method. In many ways, indeed, the affable 'Buff' looked to his senior assistants for guidance, and Combermere came to be largely run in these days by Collymore, Gibbons, Pilgrim, Williams and Webster.[32]

The age of Armstrong, for all his legendary shortcomings as a teacher and a disciplinarian (in which capacities he was notoriously inferior to Burton and Cox), was nevertheless an age of triumph for Combermere. It marked a degree of expansion totally unprecedented in the history of Barbadian education. From Cox, Armstrong inherited a roll of 240 in 1934. In 1936 alone, there were 75 new admissions, lifting the student body beyond 300 for the first time.[33]

Conditions became increasingly intolerable as the new numbers were still restricted to accommodation initially designed for 110. By 1940, the enrolment had grown to 330, and then it suddenly leapt to 418 by September 1942. Within eight years, under Armstrong, Combermere had almost multiplied itself by two.[34] The enormity of this phenomenon can perhaps best be appreciated by comparing the Combermere experience with that of the Lodge School, where the enrolment did not exceed 200 until 1943.[35] Even at Harrison College the attendance rose from 278 in 1934 to 405 only in 1942.[36]

This astonishing influx, occurring as it did during a prolonged economic slump, baffled both the legislature and the governing body. They were reluctant to impose restrictions on enrolment and yet were unable to finance the necessary expansion and renovation of buildings. For many years, therefore, Armstrong plaintively, but in vain, called upon them for adequate accommodation.[37] During the first term of 1936-37, when it had become physically impossible to house more than 300 bodies in the school, the governing body decided to rent one of the buildings of the Girls' Industrial Union (GIU) nearby, at the rate of $25 per month, in order to provide three extra classrooms. The cost was somewhat high, and the inconvenience was certainly great, but the GIU refused to renew the lease at the end of that year.[38] This produced the *ad hoc* decision to build a temporary wooden structure on the school grounds to accommodate about 100 students. A local contractor, J.T.C. Ramsay, was thus employed to erect the "Cow Shed", as it came to be called, for £456 in the summer of 1937.[39] When the enrolment outran the "Cow Shed" in 1938, the governing body was given permission to use the abandoned shop formerly occupied by the old railway foreman. This building, euphemistically called "Sayers' Court" by the boys, was adapted for classroom use by Ramsay in 1938; and then H.W. Clarke, another contractor, was hired to build some additional rooms in 1939. But still the problems of space and comfort remained defiantly unsolved.[40]

In the face of Armstrong's vigorous complaints, the governing body decided, in 1940, to establish a small committee to investigate the site carefully, prepare a list of all the things that had to be done, and offer an estimate on their cost. The committee was forced to the conclusion "that the present conditions at the Combermere School are appalling, and are a blot on the Education system of this Island".⁴¹ But when H.W. Clarke duly reported that he could effect most of the necessary repairs for $3,188, the governing body still questioned the wisdom of spending so much money to renovate buildings that they might eventually have to abandon altogether.⁴²

Combermere thus laboured under unspeakable difficulties during Armstrong's time. There was too little room for the rapidly expanding student body; the buildings were in a state of disrepair; benches, desks, chairs, and all kinds of furniture were constantly in short supply; and the governing body often seemed indifferent to the headmaster's appeals. Occasionally, he authorized repairs on his own initiative, and spent petty sums of money before they were formally approved by the governing body. This elicited mild rebukes, from time to time, from M.T.G. Mahon, the secretary/treasurer of the Education Board. Mahon, however, sent Armstrong a much more acrid note in 1938 when the latter had spent $40 more than the governing body had initially granted to complete the boys' bicycle shed. He warned the headmaster that "this is the last occasion on which [the governing body] will pay any expenditure incurred without their sanction. They ask that in future you will be careful to first obtain their authority for, before incurring, any expenditure in connection with the school".⁴³

When Armstrong was on leave in 1937, Collymore, as acting headmaster, complained to the governing body about the lack of seating accommodation for the staff. He observed that there were only eight chairs available throughout the school, and pointed out the necessity for eighteen more, including one in each of the form rooms. But the chairman could only approve the immediate purchase of five rush-bottomed chairs of pine for nine shillings each. He could not authorize the purchase of the other thirteen before consulting with his colleagues.⁴⁴ There was a perennial shortage of funds and Combermere's more urgent needs were seldom promptly met.

By far the worst feature of these makeshift arrangements was the infamous "Cow Shed". The galvanized roofing not only accentuated the midday heat but made the teacher altogether inaudible when it rained. The raindrops beat so noisily upon the roof that other sounds could not be heard. The full effect of heat and rain upon the school was never fully appreciated by the public until the memorable Speech Day of 1941 when the elements made a mockery of the proceedings—to Armstrong's unbridled glee.[45] Thereafter, everyone made a more concerted effort to improve the situation.

It was as early as 1936 that the governing body recommended to the legislature that the old Weymouth Estate should be bought and a totally new and more spacious school established there for the student body of 500 which Armstrong was already envisaging for the early 1940s.[46] But Armstrong himself was not altogether enthusiastic about uprooting the school from its birthplace. He thought that the necessary additions and renovations could be done on the original site merely by purchasing about four or five acres near the old railway tracks, leasing all the deanery lands on the Combermere side of the river, obtaining the abandoned railway land and workshop, and readjusting the old right of way. These measures would not only provide enough space for new buildings but would also permit Combermere at long last the opportunity to enjoy its own playing fields. By shifting Queen's College further away to the deanery lands, both schools could be cheaply renovated and modernized, especially if prison labour could be had for the purpose. Such a policy, in Armstrong's opinion, would be much more rational as well as economical in the long run.[47]

Moving to Weymouth

Armstrong's suggestions were neglected. The government went ahead with the idea of purchasing Weymouth. Thus Combermere was provided with twelve and a half acres of space, including eight and a half for playing fields. Having finally outgrown its original headquarters on Constitution Hill, Combermere moved into its new home on Roebuck Street at the end of 1943. The first Weymouth term began on 18 January 1944 with Armstrong still at the helm, and the new building was officially opened by the governor, Sir Henry Grattan Bushe, in an impressive ceremony on 21 July that year. The new school was designed to cater to more than 500 pupils, and by September 1944 there were already 509 on its roll.[48]

When Combermere left Constitution Hill and bequeathed the whole site to Queen's College, Mrs Effie Jane Corbin, the headmistress, was appalled by the condition of her new forms. She discovered that several repairs and renovations were necessary, and some rooms were hardly habitable. The upstairs portion of the main school needed plastering and whitewashing, the woodwork needed to be painted, and many windows and doors had to be replaced. Armstrong reminded the governing body that, as far back as 1936, he had been complaining vainly about such shabbiness. They had refused to spend money on buildings shortly to be abandoned and now the situation was much worse. He could not, therefore, hold himself responsible for the deplorable state of the school which he was now handing over to the girls.[49]

'Froggie' Gibbons continued to believe, until his death in 1990, that a good deal of Combermere's suffering in those days sprang directly from snobbery, racism and élitism. The school had become, in the 1930s, essentially an institution for lower middle class Barbadians and was now dominated by the black majority in a society still run by a minority of rich white families. He felt that Combermere's pleas were generally ignored because it was then a school "despised". Cox and Armstrong had made several requests for a suitable fence or boundary to protect the school against invasion by the denizens of the district. Nothing was done by the governing body or by the legislature to remedy the situation; but a huge seven-foot wall suddenly sprang into existence to protect Queen's College from the neighbours as soon as Combermere departed. Combermere, indeed, would not have been expelled from its original home at all had it been catering to the children of the élite. The buildings should have been renovated and extended on the deanery lands, as Armstrong had suggested, and Queen's College should have been relocated instead. Gibbons was convinced that such shabby treatment would never have been meted out to the first-grade schools. Gibbons was probably right. His view was supported by the comments of others of his generation and generally reflects the ethos of that time. Combermere had to wait again for several years to receive suitable boundaries both at Weymouth in the 1950s and at Waterford in the following decade.[50]

Division 1 Cricket Champions, 1940–41:
Back Row–L to R, *C.G. Alleyne, A. F. Ishmael, F.G. Thomas, J.H. Lucas, C.O.B. Crick.* Seated–L to R, *Mr. J.E.D. Sealy, Mr. S. O'L. Gittens, H.G. Brewster (Captain), Mr. L.L. Gittens.* Front Row–L to R, *F.M. Worrell, G.H. Sealy.*

In spite of Armstrong's indolence and general lack of administrative skills, Combermere performed very creditably both in the classroom and on the playground. Academic results were generally satisfactory during this period, which also proved to be the golden age in Combermerian sports. Thanks to the all-round excellence of Harold Brewster and C.B. Forde, Combermere won the interschool athletic championship for the first time in 1936 and proceeded to win three more titles in the next four years.[51] In 1940-41, Combermere also won the first division cricket championship—the only time it has ever done so.[52] Many Old Combermerians still remember that team very fondly indeed and are prepared to argue that it is one of the most powerful ever to be assembled by any school. It included Harold Brewster (captain),

Combermere School Cadet Corps, camping in Grenada 1939

Charles Alleyne, C.O'B. Crick, Alan F. Ishmael, Johnny Lucas, Harry Sealy, Frank Thomas, and Frank Worrell. It was bolstered by two members of the staff, Stanton O'C. Gittens and Derek Sealy, both of whom had had intercolonial cricket experience. Lionel Gittens, another assistant master, also played regularly for the school. In later years, Crick, Lucas, Thomas and Worrell were to gain selection on Barbadian cricket teams; and Worrell, of course, went on to captain the West Indies team during the early 1960s before being knighted for his services to the game.[53]

It is almost impossible to explain this remarkable flourishing of Combermere's extracurricular activity. The school, after all, still lacked adequate playing fields. But it is useful to record that Armstrong cleared the old "marl-hole" and removed some of Burton's trees, at his own expense, to find some playing space for his boys during the 1930s.[54] He also appointed Derek Sealy to the staff in 1936, in opposition to the wishes of some members of the governing body who argued that Sealy should first upgrade his qualifications beyond a junior LCC Certificate.[55] Armstrong wanted him mainly to provide inspiration to Combermere's cricketers, and Sealy continued to represent the school even when it was illogically demoted to the second division after having dominated the first.

In seeking an explanation for this Combermere phenomenon, it is necessary to look beyond the walls of the school itself. The period of Armstrong's administration coincided with that wonderful burst of Black energy which produced, among other things, the Barbados Labour Party (BLP) and the Barbados Workers' Union (BWU). The gradual rise of the coloured and black families during that first painful century which followed the abolition of slavery culminated in the establishment of such liberal newspapers as the *Herald*, edited by Clennell Wilsden Wickham in the early 1920s and the *Barbados Observer*, founded by Wynter Crawford in 1936. It was this new radical press which brought increasing pressure to bear upon the white aristocracy. The radicals kept alive the fear that, unless progressive reforms were enacted, the multitude might explode into outright rebellion. These fears appeared to be confirmed by the widespread unrest and disaffection which engulfed the whole of the Caribbean during the late 1930s. The athletic and academic triumphs of Combermerians between 1934 and 1946 must be seen, then, in this context. They were an integral part of a remarkable Black renaissance.

An Assessment of Armstrong's Role

After supervising the transition from Constitution Hill to Roebuck Street, Armstrong appears to have lost his verve. He had been able to cope with a small staff of about a dozen and an enrolment of approximately 250, but he seems to have been overwhelmed by the magnitude of the Weymouth assignment. By 1946, the school had grown to more than 550 students and the staff had risen to 24, in contrast to the 10 of 1934.[56] The members of the governing body lost their confidence in Armstrong's ability to control a school of this size and dynamism. They encouraged him to resign as soon as he reached the age of 65. He was promptly superannuated in April 1946 and a stronger personality was deliberately sought to replace him.

When the director of education was discussing the advertisement for a new Combermere headmaster, he told the secretary of the West India Committee in London that the post was a "key" one. "What we really want," he remarked, ". . . is a man of strong character and personality who can pull together a school of 500 boys, in fine buildings with a good playing field, which has rather got out of hand because the present headmaster is weak and the staff is young and inexperienced". He would therefore put character and experience ahead of high academic distinction.[57] By 1946, Bert Alkins, Stanton Gittens, H.G. Hutchinson and Derek Sealy had all gone. H.L. Goddard, 'Fab' Hoyos, G.B. Hunte and Fred Skinner had arrived in the mid-1930s, and left shortly thereafter. There was still a solid nucleus of the old guard, including Collymore, Corbin, Gibbons, Pilgrim, Williams and Webster, but they were now completely swamped by the large number of young appointees, such as Harold Brewster, Cleophas Drakes, Gladstone Holder, Harry Sealy, Chalmer St Hill, George Solomon, Bruce St John and Billy Wickham, whom Armstrong had had to bring in since 1942.[58] It is interesting to note that the monthly packet for all the members of the Combermere staff exceeded £200 for the first time in November 1934, when Armstrong himself was the only graduate among them. By January 1946, there were three degreed members of staff and the total monthly cost to the governing body had risen to some £503. That is a telling measure of Combermere's growth between 1934 and 1946.

Thus the Combermere of Roebuck Street in 1946 was substantially different, at least from the point of view of size and manageability, from the school which Armstrong had inherited from Cox. He himself had effected a number of moderate changes. He not only abolished the preparatory form in 1936, but eventually put an end to the sixth form also. He reverted to the practice, which Burton had abandoned, of entering students for the junior Cambridge School Certificate in the fourth form and preparing the best candidates to write the senior Cambridge in the fifth.

The Armstrong reforms included the rudimentary foundations for the bookstore and the school canteen which became vital Combermerian institutions later on.[59] It was Armstrong, too, who reintroduced music to Combermere, after it had disappeared from the curriculum at the very beginning of Burton's administration. He appointed Gerald Hudson, an accomplished organist and pianist, as a visiting instructor, paying him out of the Games Fund in 1935, over the mild objections of the governing body.[60] He initiated the 9 a.m. start to the school day which had formerly begun at 10 a.m.[61] He had invited the parents' comments on this proposal but went ahead with the idea even though the majority of the respondents were totally opposed to it. He also changed the official school year to correspond with the regular year after the Cambridge examinations had been shifted from July to December.[62]

On the whole, then, the Armstrong legacy was an important one. On the surface, he was the living caricature of the comic country parson, but beneath that deceptive exterior, he was capable enough to lead Combermere through a very difficult stage of its evolution. He was also surprisingly tough on occasion. In 1936, for instance, when he wanted to get rid of H.G. Hutchinson, he did so by the simple expedient of abolishing the preparatory form. The unfortunate Hutchinson was thus dismissed even though the school was then in the midst of a spectacular expansion and Armstrong was desperately searching for new teachers. While it might have become

Rev. A.E. Armstrong and his staff, 1942

necessary to remove a teacher whom the headmaster considered incompetent, it was nevertheless a sad mistake to get rid of the *prep* and Armstrong's successor was left with the task of restoring it almost as soon as the 'Buff' had left.

Fortunately, some of Armstrong's appointees proved very durable indeed and the school came to be well served by such assistant masters as Gordon Bell (1945-54), Ralph Brathwaite (1944-68), Dudley Brooker (1936-61), Cleophas Drakes (1944-54), Lionel Gittens (1937-58), Dennis Goddard (1938-61), Gladstone Holder (1944-59), Colin Moore (1939-50), Ralph Perkins (1937-70), Harry Sealy (1943-83), Chalmer St Hill (1943-59), Bruce St John (1943-63), and Billy Wickham (1942-69).

Armstrong deserved the tribute which the CSOBA paid him after his death in 1963, when it instituted the Armstrong Memorial Prize.[63] It is also fitting that one of the houses at the school, Set A, was named after him. It was Armstrong, after all, who undertook a major overhaul of the house and prefect system and introduced a fourth set (D) in 1938.[64] The historian is faced with enormous difficulty in attempting to evaluate the role of Armstrong in the evolution of Combermere. There is considerable evidence of his personal shortcomings and his reputation was by no means an enviable one. The surviving members of his staff continue to insist that the majority of important decisions were actually made by the small group of senior teachers whom his predecessors had appointed. The general feeling is that, had it not been for Frank Collymore's sagacity and guidance, the school would have fallen apart completely. Even if these views are correct, it has to be said that Armstrong had to assume full responsibility for the decisions taken and he could just as easily have decided not to heed the suggestions of his lieutenants. He administered the school at a time of great national, regional and global turmoil and worldwide economic depression. Yet, between 1934 and 1946, Combermere's enrolment more than doubled, offering greater access to Blacks. It was in Armstrong's time, in fact, that Combermere became more truly reflective of the wider community's ethnic composition as the majority of its students as well as staff members were now Black and Coloured. The school improved its academic performance and achieved excellence in extracurricular endeavours. Even if the headmaster was an easygoing parson, it is clear that he was endowed with vision and accomplished a great deal, often in the face of resistance on the part of his own governing body.

The twenty years which followed Burton's retirement saw Combermere emerge as the largest secondary school in Barbados. Cox and Armstrong consolidated the work of Burton and Speed and gave Major Cecil Noott firm foundations upon which to operate in the 1950s. If the school has retained a fine reputation over the years, those two headmasters certainly ought to share in the credit. They served at a time of unusual excitement in Barbadian history when the lower middle classes were aggressively searching for means to curtail the privileges of the small élite and to bring an end to Anglo-Saxon forms of domination. The majority of Barbadian black families then looked upon academic qualifications as an avenue of escape from an unhappy past and an uncertain present. Hence the frantic search for secondary education during the interwar period.

Under Cox and Armstrong, Combermere became the most popular choice of Barbadian parents because of, among other things, its enviable reputation for practical teaching. Combermere's fees were also more affordable, as they had remained static at £5 per year ever since 1879, as compared with the £15 still being charged by the first grade schools. In addition, Combermere because of its location remained the most accessible of all the second-grade schools as Alleyne, Coleridge, Foundation and Parry were still being plagued by transportation difficulties.

If the student body at Combermere grew so dramatically after 1930, this is really because of the acute shortage of spaces in secondary schools at that time. For all its much vaunted obsession with literacy, Barbados still had too few secondary schools to satisfy the needs of a population of about 190,000. It is by no means astonishing, then, that accommodation on Constitution Hill proved so pitifully inadequate in the 1930s.

Chapter Four

THE AGE OF NOOTT
1946-1961

The Combermere governing body's determination to find a strong personality to replace the easygoing Armstrong led them to select an energetic Welsh soldier in 1946. Major Cecil Noott was chosen from among approximately 150 applicants (including more than 100 from the United Kingdom), largely because of his relative youthfulness and his excellent war record in Burma. The keen interest in the position, which also attracted no fewer than twenty-five applications from Canada, was largely the result of the reasonable terms which Howard Hayden, the director of education, was prepared to offer: £750 per annum basic salary, a rent free unfurnished house on the school's premises, a pension equivalent to that offered in the colonial civil service, and moving expenses up to £200. Hayden agreed that Noott was the one most likely to have the necessary strength of will and character to administer a growing and dynamic school with several untrained and inexperienced teachers and more than 500 rambunctious boys.[1]

Born on 2 May 1906, Cecil Noott received his early education at the Haverfordwest Grammar School in Pembrokeshire (Dyfed). At the University College of Wales at Aberystwyth he achieved a first-class honours B.A. in 1929 and a Diploma in Education in 1930. From 1930 to 1936 he taught at the Holgate Grammar School in Barnsley, Yorkshire, where he was the master in charge of advanced courses in modern languages, and during which time he also spent a year in Germany as an exchange teacher. Noott then served during

Major C.E. Noott, Headmaster 1946-61

1936 to 1939 as senior modern languages master at the Herbert Strutt School in Belper, Derbyshire. Meanwhile, having joined the Territorial Army, he became a commissioned officer in 1932. Noott participated actively in the Second World War, serving first as battery commander during the Battle of Britain and then as major on the Headquarters Intelligence Staff in South East Asia. During the war, he travelled extensively in Burma, Ceylon, India and most of Europe.[2]

These were very impressive credentials. Still only forty, Major Noott came to Barbados as a very fine scholar and a reputable military leader. At this time, however, many Barbadians were beginning to feel disturbed by the continuing practice of importing Anglo-Saxons to administer local institutions. 'Fab' Hoyos, who had himself taught briefly at Combermere during Armstrong's tenure, wrote a scathing indictment of Noott's appointment in 1946. Under the pseudonym of 'Vindex', he took the governing body to task for bringing in a total stranger to take charge of a vitally important school when so many qualified Barbadians were available for the post. In fact, it was well known that W.A. Farmer and A.R.V. Newsam, two of Hoyos's colleagues on the Lodge School staff and who were later to become headmasters of that school, had both applied for the Combermere headship. Had their application been successful, either one of them would have doubled his salary at once since graduates in those days received between £250 and £400 per annum and could reach a maximum of £550 only if they possessed a teacher's diploma as well.[3]

The choice of Noott, however, proved a very fortunate one indeed. He at once took charge of the school in the same way perhaps as he would have done a regiment. His important memorandum on school organization, dated 11 October 1946, reveals the confidence and authority with which he immediately spoke. Addressing the assistant masters, Noott expressed extreme disappointment at "the casual way in which the boys and some members of the staff responded to the school routine at 0925 this morning". He felt "very strongly on the question of the staff setting an example of briskness and punctuality". Rather than resort to a policy of repression, however, he would prefer to employ the democratic principle and encourage the senior pupils to play an active role in the improvement of conduct and discipline.[4]

It was this concern for discipline and deportment that led Noott to recommend a general overhaul of the house and prefect system. The division of the school into sets, he observed, "offers a ready-made framework of decentralization". He would thus expand the house system already in existence. The four houses would continue to be known as Sets A, B, C and D, retaining their traditional names of Armstrong, Burton, Cox and Speed. They would preserve their distinctive colours: blue, red, gold and green respectively. Every staff member, except the headmaster and the second master, would become attached to a house and each house was to be administered by a senior master and one of the other teachers. All the boys were to be allocated to a house and each boy had the right to request a specific membership. The house lists were to be adequately publicized and each house was to have its own notice board.[5]

More importantly, Noott recommended that each house should have its own corps of six prefects and enjoy the right of choosing its own captain and vice captain. Assisted by the corps of set prefects and officers, the staff would then choose the captain and vice captain of the whole school. These elections were to be approved by the headmaster. Noott also invited the corps of officers to draw up a constitution or charter for the prefects, defining their privileges as well as their obligations, and to submit it for his approval. Hence the drafting of the famous Prefects' Charter in 1946 which has remained in operation ever since, with but minor amendments to accommodate the changes inherent in the exodus to Waterford.[6] The staff agreed with these proposals, after meeting with the headmaster "not later than 15 October", and with the detailed programme of prefects' rights and duties which became so familiar to every Combermerian during the 1950s: duty rosters, etc., with two prefects becoming responsible for patrolling the corridors and conducting the detention classes each week. Thus did Noott invite twenty-six senior boys to participate in the important business of supervising the student body. This was an extraordinary proceeding in post-war Barbados. Even today, prefects are still selected for the students in some schools because the teachers believe that pupils simply cannot be trusted to behave responsibly and to develop their own leadership skills. The democratic election of prefects at Combermere in 1946 was thus an important landmark in Barbadian education.

To cope with increasing numbers, this house system was overhauled again in 1950. Noott now created two additional sets, E and F, and named them Webster (the venerable 'Goot' having just retired) and Weymouth. He put Gordon Bell and Neilton Seale in charge of set E, and placed set F under the care of Jack Adams and Gladstone Holder. Each set was now to be administered by two assistant masters, one captain, a vice captain, a prefect and three sub prefects. There were thus thirty-eight student officers at Combermere during the 1950s to satisfy Noott's belief that the optimum ratio of officers to the rank and file should be 1:15.[7] In 1952, Noott increased the authority of the school captain and vice captain by placing them in charge of the whole prefect corps and permitting the school captain to flog junior miscreants for serious infractions. Earle Newton, the school captain during 1952-53, found this assignment somewhat distasteful and delegated the vice captain, Harold Crichlow (now the dean of St Michael's Cathedral), to fulfil it. After Newton's departure, Crichlow continued the practice, rather indifferently, when he himself was school captain during 1953-54. His successor, Keith A.P. Sandiford, abandoned it altogether. But for some years thereafter, the school captain was one of the most feared and respected individuals at the school. He was considered by the student body at large a much more authoritative figure than most of the junior assistant masters. This was clearly emphasized in recent interviews with a number of Old Combermerians of that period. To encourage the prefects to perform their assignments with greater zeal, Crichlow introduced a Challenge Cup for the most efficient house in 1953. This competition, however, did not survive the exodus to the Garrison in 1955.[8]

The resurrection of the house system went far towards improving the general conduct of Combermerians after 1946. The prefects ensured the gradual destruction of the old cruel practice of "christening" the new boys; and incessant bullying, which had become a major problem in Armstrong's later years, came virtually to an end. Here, Noott showed his concern for the younger children and his determination to provide a peaceful climate and an orderly atmosphere. The purpose of the new house system was to provide improved discipline since it was administered by the boys themselves. Small units also meant better opportunities for guidance and support. Younger pupils would no longer feel bewildered in a growing school. The establishment of a sixth form in 1952 also gave senior prefects much greater authority and stature. Previously, the senior boys had left Combermere School around seventeen years of age. Now they were allowed to spend two more years at school. Prefects tended therefore to be more mature and more responsible during the age of Noott. His belief in an orderly and purposeful climate and his concern for his students led him to undertake these changes. The recent literature on effective schools stresses the need for the creation of such an environment and thus helps to enhance Noott's reputation.[9]

The Major's Long-Term Goals

The new headmaster was not only concerned with sets and houses. He was far more interested in long-term goals. He began indeed by mapping out an entirely new strategy for the school and presenting the governing body with his first five-year plan in 1947, after watching Combermere in operation for one term. He was determined to put his stamp on the institution by revamping both its administration and its curriculum.[10] In January 1947, he allocated 106 students to the three first forms to give them two years of general training before dividing them into streams. The two main streams after 1949 would become the academic and commercial/vocational. By 1951, the 5A would be ready to take the Cambridge School Certificate, and the 5C would be preparing for the LCC examinations. The older and less able boys whom Noott had inherited from Armstrong would be "canalized into Alpha Forms" and coached in some of the LCC subjects before reaching the school-leaving age. They had previously been left to drift through the school until it was decided to ask them to leave. Noott now gave them something to work towards. But this interim policy was to lapse after 1950. Thereafter, the five-year plan would become fully operative. The preparatory form for underage pupils which Armstrong had abolished in 1936 was also reintroduced.

Noott at once recommended a drastic overhaul of the school's internal administration. He began by delegating more authority to the second master, Frank Collymore, and appointing Lionel Gittens master in charge of the junior school. Combermere was accordingly divided into two administrative halves in 1947, since the new headmaster felt that the administrative methods of the 1930s were totally inappropriate for a school of its size and complexity. Through these strategic moves, Noott allowed much authority and power to two individuals, giving a tremendous boost to their morale, while releasing himself for further planning and other professional activity. It is now universally agreed that delegation and staff development are vital. Noott remained committed to these principles. He consistently tried to provide his teachers with opportunities for growth on the job and with generous leave conditions for study.

Noott called also for a revision of staffing policy. He found only two university graduates among his assistants when he arrived, and he was determined to increase that number. He expressed dismay, too, at the ratio of masters to pupils which was then close to 1:24. He thought that the school should aim at 1:21 or 1:20. He therefore requested four additional teachers, insisting that "a definition of Staff-establishment in terms of staff ratios is the only adequate means of enabling me to cater for special Forms or groups—whether for School Certificate or catering for backward boys". His conclusion, in short, was that important curriculum reforms could be implemented only by an immediate increase of permanent staff.[11]

As for the curriculum itself, the new headmaster planned, as soon as possible, to introduce art, history, typewriting and woodwork. He was determined to expand the curriculum in such a way as to provide a meaningful education for a fuller life. A basic characteristic of effective heads is their concern with curriculum and instructional matters. In Noott's judgement, no single subject was ultimately as important as history; art was an indispensable medium of education; woodwork had vocational value and also allowed pupils a medium of self-expression; and typewriting should long ago have been provided for, given Combermere's tradition of preparing candidates for the LCC Certificate. These changes would entail the purchase of new equipment, including at least twelve typewriters, ten woodwork benches, and twenty-four art desks. Noott recognized that these items were expensive but, in projecting his vision for the school, he insisted that the absence of these vital subjects from the school curriculum was a fundamental defect that had to be remedied promptly.[12]

These far-reaching plans for broadening the Combermere curriculum were never completely abandoned. Noott continued, Speech Day after Speech Day, to demand a more balanced curriculum. In 1950, for example, he expressed the hope that Combermere would soon become a technical as well as academic centre. He was sure that the school could contribute to the community in many ways and argued that carpentry (for instance) was not a demeaning occupation.[13] In 1952, he prayed that Combermere would develop into something much more than a School Certificate factory and play a more vigorous role in all areas of Barbadian life.[14] And, in 1953, he made another plaintive appeal for the long promised science laboratory for which the school was still patiently waiting.[15] Such ideas for broadening the curriculum at a time when curricula were mainly classical and traditional provide further evidence of Noott's educational vision. His concern was to provide for the all-round development of the student and in this he had, on the whole, a good measure of success.

If a few of these dreams came to nothing, it was not for want of trying. The idea of a technical stream was much discussed until a separate Technical Institute was eventually opened elsewhere in Barbados. For many years, too, Noott persevered with the idea of establishing a commercial stream in the hope that some day Combermere would offer advanced level instruction in this area. By 1949 the post was still vacant although the school had already been frantically advertising for a commercial specialist for years. Hence the prevailing mood of desperation when Carl S. Herkes was appointed that year. He came, however, with too little intelligence and too many faked qualifications and had to be summarily dismissed in November 1950 as soon as his fraud was exposed. A more careful examination of his credentials would certainly have avoided such embarrassment, since he obviously claimed too many different kinds of degrees for so young an applicant.[16] Colin O'Kiersey came in September 1952, found the task of establishing a commercial stream beyond him, and left unlamented at the end of one academic year.[17] Appointed in October 1956, L.F. Emblem complained about the inadequacy of his salary and hastily retreated to Britain, whence he had come, in April 1957.[18] T.C. Hill, who was appointed amidst great controversy in 1958 (when local newspapers accused him of fraudulently drawing salaries from both Combermere and Harrison College), also proved a failure.[19] Thus Noott ultimately had to admit defeat in this matter of establishing a commercial stream for his boys.

The Stamp of Noott

He was much more successful, however, in his valiant quest for the creation of a science stream at Combermere. But that task, too, was much more frustrating than Noott could ever have anticipated. In 1949, he encouraged Cleo Drakes to upgrade his qualifications by attending the University College of the West Indies (UCWI) at Mona, Jamaica. Drakes was offered attractive study leave terms: one year at full pay, two more at half. He graduated in 1952 but returned to find that Combermere had not yet been provided with a science laboratory. He soon departed for Harrison College. Thus the rewards from Combermere's financial investment, as Noott sadly observed, were reaped by another institution.[20] Advertisements for Drakes's replacement bore no immediate fruit, but the teaching of general science at Combermere was finally begun in 1956 when the school received yeoman service from James Seers, an American Fullbright scholar, who unfortunately had to go back to the United States in 1957.[21] Noott then had to wait until 1958 for the return of Eustace Taitt, another young assistant master, whom he had first appointed to the staff in 1949. Taitt, an Old Harrisonian who later joined the physics department on the Cave Hill campus of the University of the West Indies, now came back as a qualified physicist after three years of study leave at the UCWI.[22] The headmaster could look forward at long last with some optimism to the opening of the new science laboratory at Waterford in 1959.[23] The school for many years continued to lack adequate or proper equipment, but it was chiefly due to Noott's perseverance and determination that Combermere became actively involved in the teaching of science.

Noott's stamp on the Combermere curriculum is clearly indelible. He promptly introduced the teaching of history, appointing first J. Cameron (now Sir James) Tudor in January 1947 and then Ronald G. Hughes in 1950 to teach this vital subject that the school, inexplicably, had failed to offer previously. Hughes was an alumnus of the Lodge School and had left Combermere in 1946 after teaching there for one year under Armstrong. He had just completed his B.A. honours degree at the University of Toronto. He immediately made history one of Combermere's most important subjects and taught it with considerable success until 1958. History was one of the first subjects offered by the school at advanced level in 1953. Four of the five candidates passed it that inaugural year. It was also the first subject in which Combermere achieved an advanced level distinction (in 1955).[24]

As he had promised, Noott also introduced typewriting, but it never quite made the same impact as did art, which came with the fortunate hiring of Karl Broodhagen, the celebrated sculptor, in 1949. Born in what was then British Guiana on 4 July 1909, 'Broodie' had already established a reputation for his art and sculpture. He had come to Barbados in his youth and was earning his living as a tailor in Bridgetown, at a time when the livelihood of a Caribbean artist was a most precarious one. In his own quiet, inimitable fashion, he established the art room as one of the liveliest centres of the school. As Noott often admitted, the art room became the haven for "many a dullard and a dolt" who found the other aspects of the curriculum much too tedious.[25] But other gifted students of art honed their skills in this atmosphere, and Karl's own son, Virgil, who has since made quite a name for himself as a distinguished artist in Canada, became (in 1961) the first student in the Eastern Caribbean to pass an examination in sculpting at advanced level. Broodhagen has remained on the staff to this day, despite his official retirement in 1969 at the age of sixty. His is simply too valuable a skill and cannot easily be replaced. He has taught most of the leading artists and sculptors in Barbados and still himself remains (in 1995) perhaps the most outstanding modern artist in the Caribbean. His appointment by Noott represented one of the major landmarks in the history of Combermere as it certainly added an important dimension to the school's cultural life. Unfortunately, however, Broodhagen was most shabbily treated by the Education Board which refused to grant him a graduate salary or to recognize the full value of his Goldsmith College of Art diploma—in spite of the constant appeals from the headmaster and the governing body throughout the 1950s. 'Broodie' accepted this maltreatment philosophically and continued his labours to make the art room one of the main centres of attraction at all of Combermere's Speech Days since 1950.[26]

Even more glorious has been the history of Combermerian music. For many years vocal music had been encouraged by Gerald Hudson, who helped with the school choir, and 'Graffie' Pilgrim, under whom the famous Glee Club had prospered. But Noott was anxious to introduce some kind of instrumental music to the school and toyed with the notion of importing an English expert for this purpose. From this course he was soon deflected by some members of the governing body who urged him to utilize the enormous gifts of a local virtuoso, James A. 'Shakespeare' Millington, who was then perhaps the most accomplished violinist in the West Indies.[27] Noott agreed to give the latter an opportunity to display his talents as a teacher and never had cause to regret that decision. Millington was appointed a visiting master in September 1949, and Combermere has never really been the same since. He brought an infectious zeal and intensity to the school which affected far more than just its music. He established the violin as one of the most prized features of the Combermere tradition. His pupils gave countless recitals and earned the most fulsome praise for almost forty years. Combermere's music results have consistently been very good, and Jimmy's Boys (as Noott called them) stole the show in virtually all the school's functions until Millington himself died in 1987.

Millington's value to Combermere was recognized from as early as the 1950s, when he was appointed to the permanent staff on the same basis as an honours graduate. He officially retired in 1962, at the age of sixty, but like Broodhagen, continued in an acting capacity for several years after that. Such skills as his are really irreplaceable.[28] Altogether, Millington gave the school thirty-eight years of unbroken service and thus ranks with Webster behind only Collymore (54), Wilson (46), Broodhagen (46), Williams (42) and Sealy (40) among all Combermere teachers in length of tenure. On 22 January 1989, the CSOSA staged an ambitious and impressive First Annual James Millington Memorial Concert at the Frank Collymore Hall. This was an eminently fitting tribute to one of Combermere's truly outstanding teachers.

At Roebuck Street, in the early 1950s, Noott also established a very impressive geography room in the hope of demonstrating the enormous value of physical geography.[29] He promoted the teaching of geography at the advanced level and finally established this discipline as one of Combermere's strongest. Dennis Goddard, who took charge of the geography room in its infancy, was the specialist who replaced Webster as the senior geography master in 1950. Himself an Old Combermerian, Goddard had first joined the staff on 1 May 1938. He was destined to remain at Combermere until 1961 when marriage took him to Trinidad.[30]

Noott also felt that a successful secondary school could not function effectively without a substantial library and its own bookstore. His immediate objective in 1946 was to acquire about 6,000 volumes for the school library and to extend the lending system to the entire school to encourage the juniors in particular to cultivate the habit of reading. By 1950, the Combermere collection had come close to 3,000 and the library was prospering under the capable guidance of Chalmer St Hill, an Old Combermerian who had placed first in the island in the Cambridge School Certificate examinations in 1936 and whom Armstrong had originally appointed on 1 September 1943.[31] When the acquisitions eventually outgrew the single classroom which housed the library at Weymouth, Noott persuaded the governing body to extend the library by demolishing the partition between it and the adjacent classroom.[32] By 1951, the school library now occupied two full classrooms. St Hill co-opted senior pupils to act as library assistants to help with the cataloguing and accessioning of new books. For a few years the school library really flourished, but its excellent stock was hard hit by the hurricane of September 1955 and subsequent grants proved inadequate to repair the damage. The school library also suffered later in that decade from the departure of St Hill and his deputy Gladstone Holder, the two assistant masters who had done most to keep it alive at Weymouth. They were attracted to the civil service by superior conditions of service. Holder went on to become Government Information Officer, while St Hill was appointed Public Librarian and administered the Barbados Public Library from 1959 until early 1980. It took a herculean effort later on to restore the school library at Waterford. It remains, however, an essential part of the Noott tradition. The creation of a sizeable library was a major development not only because of what was lacking before but because of its importance in learning and education. To devote a full-time staff member to it was truly innovative and a sign of the value that Noott placed on it.[33]

Noott also overhauled completely the rudimentary textbook scheme that Armstrong had introduced in 1943. As early as 1947, he announced plans for ordering stationery, equipment and text books for the pupils' use.[34] The governing body lent $2,112 to the new stationery scheme in 1948 when several volumes were ordered from London.[35] In 1949 the School Textbook Store was formally opened and left under the direction of G.R. Brathwaite, who remained in charge of it until his retirement in December 1968.[36] Noott's comprehensive textbook and stationery scheme was one of the significant elements of his legacy to the school. For many years it permitted Combermerians to purchase, at reasonable prices, books, stationery and equipment not readily available in Bridgetown stores. Considering that the majority of the students came from the working and lower middle classes, this scheme was of vital importance. It permitted boys to own their own books and stationery. When he later introduced a book rental scheme, he further eased the burden on poor parents. It is also much to Noott's credit that the Barbados government was to adopt such a scheme on a national basis in later years.

Noott found a school canteen already in existence. It had been opened on 16 September 1944 and was intended to be self-sufficient after a brief period of initial funding by the Education Board.[37] The canteen, in effect, was the old "Cow Shed" which had been removed from Constitution Hill.[38] Noott took a more active interest in its development by placing Lionel Gittens in charge of its accounts and promulgating an edict which forbade students from purchasing lunch from the itinerant vendors off Roebuck Street.[39] He ordered the school's gates to be closed at the break and luncheon intervals and issued "lunch passes" only to those pupils whose parents sought special permission for them to leave school during the lunch break. The canteen thus gradually became an integral feature of Combermerian life, as its attendants—Beryl, 'Grannie', Rita, Stella and Mrs. Maloney—soon established a fine rapport with the staff and the students. The canteen operated at an average annual loss of $176 and never became self-sufficient even though the attendants were poorly paid.[40] By 1958 they were threatening to quit when a Canteen Subcommittee, set up by the governing body, recommended an immediate and significant increase in their wages.[41]

The canteen at Weymouth, 1944–55

Noott left his mark even on the school hall at Weymouth. He envisaged its regular use by local performers who might also be prepared to support the school welfare fund, which he himself inaugurated in 1947.[42] He persuaded the governing body, the British Council and the Education Board to finance the hall's conversion into a modern auditorium from which the cultural life of the wider community could benefit. Voluntary subscriptions to the welfare fund in the first six months of 1947 amounted only to $83, but the school used this money to pay the school fees of two needy and deserving students and to transfer the balance (about $42) to the Games Fund.[43] So integral a part of Combermere had the hall become that it loomed large in all of the designs for the new school when the Weymouth building had to be abandoned in 1955.

Combermere profited also from Noott's interest in its cadets and scouts. With his military background, he was very keen on all cadet activity and followed very closely the fortunes of the Combermere School Cadet Company. He worked hard to erect a miniature rifle range at Weymouth in the early 1950s, and then had it removed to Waterford when the school was relocated there in 1958.[44] Among the officers commanding the Combermere School Cadet Company during Noott's tenure were Ralph Perkins, the longest serving, and Livy Goring, the most effective and efficient. Charlie Pilgrim also stepped into the breach both during this period and afterwards to provide continuity when staff changes would have caused a hiatus in the company. Goring, a member of the first sixth form, was first appointed to the staff in 1954. He served the school with great devotion for some eleven years before being seconded in 1965 to the Department of National Archives as an assistant archivist. He resigned from the Combermere staff in 1967 when he was named Consul General of Barbados at New York. He had worked especially hard during the late 1950s to make the Combermere School Cadet Company one of the most efficient in the island. This tradition was carried on by such Old Combermerians as Harold Crichlow, Deighton Maynard and Patrick Skeete.

As for scouting, Noott was himself the chairman of the publicity committee of the Island Scout Council during the 1950s when he did much to make Bob-a-Job Week a successful project. He left a full scout file in his voluminous records at Waterford which testify to his abiding interest in the scouting movement. He gave great encouragement to the Combermere Scout Troop which flourished during his regime under G.R. Brathwaite's leadership.[45] Noott's attachment to the cadets and scouts left him with a curious fondness for the wearing of uniforms, which was also an old British school tradition. He felt that uniforms did much to remove social distinctions while promoting a sense of *esprit* and belonging. He was convinced that they led to greater order and tidiness. He therefore tried his best to impose a system of compulsory school uniforms for all Combermerians but could not persuade the governing body to agree before 1951. They advised him to give the parents one year's notice, which he promptly did. He circulated a form letter announcing that the school uniform (khaki shirt and shorts, black shoes, navy hose with gold trim, and school tie) would become mandatory after April 1952. He also made arrangements with Cave, Shepherd & Co. Ltd., a local department store, to supply it.[46] Combermere had long had its unique colours and uniforms but it was Noott who first made them compulsory. Nowadays, all Barbadian secondary schools insist on the compulsory wearing of uniforms.

It was Major Noott, too, who popularized and institutionalized the famous school song, "Up and On!", which is still sung with much gusto at the school and by Old Combermerians whenever they meet. This song, apparently previously introduced, was hardly known and little used until Noott's recognition of its inspirational and symbolic value. The song itself is not original. However, its fine combination of stirring melody and dramatic lyrics instantly became a Combermere tradition. It was sung regularly during normal school time and was a *sine qua non* at all ceremonial occasions. Noott insisted that it be sung with spirit and vigour and that the words be known. The song typifies and gives expression to the total vision he had for the school. Generations of Combermerians at a reunion feel themselves closely knit together when it is sung. No assessment of Combermere School under Noott can be made without some understanding of the immense emotive force of "Up and On!"

Preserving the Athletic Tradition

Noott was also anxious to preserve the tradition of athleticism which his predecessors had fostered. He spent many long hours trying to make the new fields at Weymouth suitable for sports. Eventually, in 1952, he managed to clear away the two acres of jungle between Harrison College and Hall's Road, adjacent to the canal, to establish the hockey field for his boys. It was by no means accidental therefore that Combermere soon became the first Barbadian school to play field hockey with any seriousness or skill. The game was introduced to the school by Jack Adams, whom Noott had appointed in 1947 to teach mathematics to the upper forms after Gibbons's resignation.[47] Adams very soon produced many fine hockey players, such as Trevor Haynes, Gilbert Holder, Deighton Maynard, Cammie Newton, David Skinner and Walter Reid. During the 1950s, with the aid of such young colleagues as Carl Ince and Keith Sandiford, Adams built up that unique tradition of hockey excellence of which Combermere is still supremely proud. Ever since then, indeed, many of the leading hockey players in Barbados have been Combermerians past and present.

Combermere performed extremely well during the age of Noott in a wide range of sporting activity. His boys, for instance, not only won the interschool athletic championship in 1954, but played an exciting brand of cricket throughout that decade. Noott's role here was vitally important as it was he who appointed Frank King, the West Indian fast bowler, as head groundsman and cricket coach in the early 1950s. Later, he employed Everton Weekes, the great West Indian batsman, to coach the school on a part-time basis. He also appointed Ronnie Hughes the cricket master in 1952. Hughes, who had played cricket for the Lodge School and Wanderers in his youth, took this assignment very seriously indeed and spent many hours trying to develop the skills of Combermere's most promising youngsters. The result was that in Noott's time, Combermere produced a fine array of cricketing talent. Among the players coached by Hughes were Rawle Brancker, Victor Callender, Ossie Gill, Wesley Hall, Errie Inniss, Patrick Lashley, Francis Scott, Ralph Walker, Lionel Williams and Wilfred Wood. Of this group, four went on to gain selection for Barbados and three of them were destined to tour with West Indian teams during the 1960s; while Hall, whose wicket-keeping skills Hughes had done most to develop, surprisingly emerged as one of the world's greatest fast bowlers after leaving school. He later became a cabinet minister in the DLP governments of the 1980s and 1990s. Wood, whom Hughes appointed Combermere's cricket captain in 1953, eventually made his mark in a totally different arena. He is famous for having become the first black bishop in the Anglican Church in the United Kingdom.

An important element in the Noott tradition was the introduction of boxing as a prominent feature of physical training. Karl Broodhagen and Bruce St John did most to popularize this sport in the 1950s. St John, an Old Harrisonian, was actually one of the first Barbadians to specialise in physical education. He studied at Loughborough College before returning in 1948 to demonstrate the seriousness of a field which most Barbadians hitherto had neglected.[48] During the period of Noott's administration, it was St John and Harold Brewster, himself one of the most celebrated of Combermerian athletes, who did most to establish the tradition of serious physical education which still persists at Combermere.[49]

The Introduction of the Sixth Forms and A Levels

But Noott's greatest legacy to the school, beyond any question, was the creation of a sixth form in 1952 designed to undertake advanced level studies that had previously been possible only at the first-grade secondary schools which had traditionally catered to the white élite. The Whites and upper middle-class population had a vested interest in preserving the élite first-grade schools and saw the development of a sixth form at Combermere as encroaching on their special reserve. But Noott fought vigorously against mighty opposition for the establishment of a sixth form and it remains a major feature of the school with some 175 senior pupils today.

Noott based his decision, in 1951, on the recent changes in the policy of English universities which had just raised their matriculation requirements. He called for an immediate revision of the old scheme of government as the universities were now insisting on at least five GCE credits, including at least two at A level. "If Combermere School must stop at O Levels," Noott argued, "then it can only do so at the cost of lowering its standards". He recommended to the governing body that the school should offer A level instruction in those subjects warranted by the staff and equipment already available. He planned to select a handful of the brightest students from the form 5A which was then preparing for the Cambridge School Certificate in December. Among the subjects he felt that Combermere could then offer at the higher level were English, French, geography and history.[50]

After considerable debate, the governing body finally agreed with Noott's suggestions and persuaded the Education Board that the expansion of the curriculum in this manner could be accomplished without any additional money or men. The board reluctantly sanctioned this revolutionary programme in 1952, but with the express proviso that the school would not later demand increasing grants to implement it. Major C. Glindon Reed, the director of education, regarded the arrangement as purely temporary and urged Combermere to concentrate more on technical and commercial streams instead of competing with Harrison College and the Lodge in an academic market already glutted.[51] As late as 1954, E.C.M. Theobalds, then acting director of education, was still arguing that it was wasteful to run a sixth form at Combermere with only half a dozen students when it was so much more economical to transfer them to Harrison College next door.[52]

Notwithstanding the hesitancy of the Education Board, Noott pressed on with his plan to develop a sixth form tradition at Combermere, and was highly successful. The experiment began with five students reading French and history, in an atmosphere of great uncertainty. Within eight years, however, the sixth form had grown to forty-five taking a variety of options. The early results were most encouraging indeed. Between 1953 and 1957 alone, Combermerians gained twenty-one A level certificates in French, twenty-one in Latin, ten in history, and ten in geography.[53] In his Speech Day address in 1956, Noott was able to boast that the experiment had already produced Harold Crichlow, Livy Goring,

Earle Newton, Keith Sandiford and Neville Smith who had all joined the staff in acting capacities after leaving school, and Newton had become the first to enter university directly from the school under the new matriculation scheme.[54] In 1958, when serving as acting headmaster in Noott's absence, 'Bull' Williams observed that the sixth form had been exceedingly valuable to the life of the school, having done much to improve O level results as more fifth formers were now aiming at promotion to the sixth. He thought that the sixth form had not only contributed to the vast improvement in the discipline of the school but was also encouraging some members of staff to think more seriously in terms of upgrading their own academic qualifications.[55] By 1960, Noott himself was ready to acknowledge that the creation of the sixth form in the early 1950s was the single greatest change in the organization of Combermere School in his time.[56]

Combermere's determination to prepare its pupils for A level examinations contributed significantly to the destruction of the traditional distinction between first-grade and second-grade secondary schools in Barbados. Noott abandoned the Cambridge School Certificate as well as the LCC examinations after 1952, noting that, with the emergence of the newer and more respectable general certificates, the LCC especially no longer served a useful purpose. He aimed first at the London GCE and then at the Oxford and Cambridge syndicate to give his students an opportunity to compete for scholarships and exhibitions. Livy Goring and Keith Sandiford thus became, in 1954, the first two Combermerians to write Barbados Scholarship examination papers.[57] The school did not win one of the coveted awards—the prestigious Barbados Scholarship—until 1967, but at least Noott had the satisfaction of seeing one of his boys win a Government Exhibition to the UCWI in 1956. These decisions necessitated another change in the school year, which now had to begin in September and end in July. To facilitate the transition, Noott announced in 1951 that two terms would be added to the existing academic session.

While Major Noott did so much to modernize Combermere, there is one area in which he accomplished precious little. He had been most eager to keep alive the annual school magazine, but it perished nevertheless during the course of his administration. Only two issues appeared during the fifteen years of his headship. Noott had strongly urged the resurrection of the *Combermerian* in 1947, stressing its utility in bolstering the spirit of the school while serving as its bible and its history. As the school magazine would be read by an overseas as well as local audience, he thought it "essential therefore that it shall be of the highest quality". He struck a small subcommittee, including a chief editor, a business editor, and two sub-editors. He ruled that the chief editor should be the senior English teacher and that a bright senior pupil should be one of the sub-editors. He also felt that the School Magazine Committee should include two students and one Old Boy. While the chief editor would vet and select material, including advertisements, the business editor would arrange for printing and sales. As to content, Noott looked for form reports, set reports and games reports, written by some of the brighter students (in consultation with the form and set masters) to give them valuable experience.

Despite such careful planning, this School Magazine Committee managed to produce but a single issue, the *Combermerian 1947*, apparently under the editorship of C. DeVere Moore. Its successor met frequently a few years later and laboured mightily, under Gordon Bell's editorship, to produce a volume for 1949-50. But it involved so many headaches, delays and complications that no effort was made to publish another issue before 1956. In fact, as late as 1953, the school still owed the *Advocate* printery over $445 for bills incurred in the production of the 1949-50 volume.[58] The frenetic magazine discussions of the late 1950s all foundered on the rock of expense. Thus were Noott's fondest hopes most cruelly disappointed.[59] He was absolutely right in claiming that a magazine could serve as a vital source of information for social historians. As it was, he left only two issues, but compensated by leaving copious newspaper clippings and personal memoranda for posterity. His strong sense of history and of his own mission inspired him to leave at Waterford a host of files and memorabilia on every aspect of his life and work at Combermere School.

Major Noott's Legacy

Most of Cecil Noott's triumphs were achieved in the face of overwhelming odds. Not only did he often have to face resistance from the Education Board to some of his more ambitious programmes, but he also had to lead the school through its very unhappy phase at the Drill Hall. For many years, too, difficulties were created by the lack of definitive rules outlining the duties and responsibilities of the secretary/treasurer of the school's governing body. It was not exactly clear whether that individual was responsible solely to the governing body or partly to the headmaster himself. Thus, conflicts often arose between Noott and P.A.K. Tucker (who had succeeded M.T.G. Mahon) during 1946-47. When the latter was replaced by Miss Miriam Naomi Pindar, there was no obvious boundary between her bailiwick and that of Miss Grace Hunte, the headmaster's secretary. This led to much confusion and dissatisfaction until a small committee of the governing body produced more specific regulations in 1958.[60]

In addition, Noott had to cope, during most of his tenure, with a relatively untrained and inexperienced staff that was perpetually in a state of flux. No sooner had he arrived than Gibbons departed. Thereafter there was never any suggestion of stability. By 1961, very few of Armstrong's assistant masters were still on the Combermere staff and even some of those whom Noott himself had appointed left long before he did.[61] Replacements were difficult to find precisely because of the short sightedness of the government which continued to pay higher salaries to public servants than to teachers. As Noott lamented so bitterly in 1956, the salaries paid to graduates were too low to encourage them to remain in the teaching profession. He harshly criticized "the folly of robbing the schools to feed the expanding Civil Service" which was "insidiously eating away the standards of our Teaching Staff".[62]

The age of Noott is most closely associated with the Weymouth phase of Combermere's history. He was immensely proud of the school's new surroundings and did his best to beautify and modernize them. The huge playground was eventually levelled, suitable gates and boundaries were finally provided, trees were planted and nurtured, and the *Barbados Evening Advocate* could well remark in 1952 that the school had become one of the most modern, spacious, and beautiful throughout the Caribbean.[63] The importance of pleasant surroundings to growth and learning has often been stressed.[64] Noott himself spent long hours working on the grounds, planting trees and shrubs and pulling weeds. He also encouraged the boys to bring flowering and decorative trees and shrubs. He was a great environmentalist who believed that children should grow up in a clean and beautiful environment. When Weymouth had unfortunately to be abandoned, he tried at Waterford but had insufficient time to do much there. In fact, a senior member of staff wondered recently what the Waterford grounds would be like had Noott had more time to develop them.

But the Weymouth buildings were doomed from the very beginning, as Frank Gibbons has observed, because the advice of George Edgar Peck, the Colonial Engineer to the Director of Public Works, was unfortunately set aside. He had warned against building heavy structures on that swampy site without driving piles.[65] The school's foundations thus proved untrustworthy and the building began to collapse after the great flood of 1949. On 29 September that year, the main floor of the school hall suddenly subsided approximately six inches in its centre during the usual morning assembly. Terrified by the loud and frequent cracking noises emanating from beneath them, both boys and masters took to flight. The governing body thereupon decided to relocate the junior school until certain structural repairs could be effected. The upper school remained at Roebuck Street while the junior boys sought temporary refuge in the Queen's Park shed. Between 1950 and 1953, the school was reunited at Weymouth but the earthquake of 19 March 1953 did such severe damage to the walls of the school that the junior forms had to spend the whole academic year 1953-54 in the army huts at the Drill Hall in the Garrison. Then came the drought of 1955 which undid all the repairs of 1949 and 1953 and forced the governing body to abandon the Weymouth site altogether.[66]

Combermere then spent three long years in the proverbial wilderness. Until a new site could be found and a new school built, all the boys were shepherded into the army huts at the Drill Hall

The Hockey XI in 1960

which were by no means suitable for the purpose for which they were being used. The classes were too close together and voices from neighbouring rooms were too clearly audible. There was an acute shortage of space everywhere. The corporate life of the school suffered, the house and prefect system became virtually defunct, and the Weymouth playground was too far away to permit any meaningful physical education.[67] From September 1955 to August 1958, the school laboured under extreme difficulties. During this period, however, Combermere's examination results were satisfactory. The cadets and scouts remained alive. The students continued to participate in a wide variety of activities, performing particularly well in athletics and field hockey. Millington's violinists continued to play well, and Broodhagen's budding artists performed with their usual excellence. Such a fine record of achievement at a time of such dislocation speaks volumes for Noott's administrative genius.

It was during the Garrison phase of Combermere's existence that the government conducted another investigation of all aspects of

Barbadian education with the view of modernizing the system. This determination was reinforced by the famous Petter Report, published in 1956. G.S.V. Petter, an education expert from Britain, recommended, among several far-reaching reforms, increased salaries for all teachers, a broadening of the curriculum to escape from the stifling supremacy of the classics and modern studies, and an upgrading of teachers' skills at all levels.[68] Another report, presented by Fred Miller, a member of the school's governing body, also recommended specific changes for the new Combermere. Miller hoped to establish what he called a "multi-lateral" school at Waterford catering to more than 1,000 students and offering instruction in a variety of disciplines.[69] It was mainly in keeping with such suggestions as these that Combermere School was eventually reconstituted at Waterford.

Noott himself pressed in 1956 for the erection of a school large enough to accommodate 800 pupils in the first instance and flexible enough to cater to 1,200 which he projected for the 1960s. He stressed the need for a geography room, chemistry and general science laboratories, a book store, a large library, an elementary workshop, and a comfortable art room. But he was most concerned, as usual, with the question of staffing, insisting on an immediate increase of the establishment by as many as fifteen assistant masters, including two science teachers and one each for metal work and woodwork. He argued that five well qualified men were needed for every additional 100 students.[70] He also warned, in response to Miller's suggestions, that Combermere would need at least three years of readjustment at Waterford before embarking on ambitious schemes of expansion.[71] This important memorandum provides further evidence of Noott's vision for Combermere and his profound concern for equipment as well as personnel, which he always regarded as the two major resources for effective teaching.

When the school assembled for the first time at Waterford in September 1958, it already had accommodation for 720 students and included many of the features for which Noott had specifically asked. He was thus able to report, during the official opening ceremony on 11 December 1959, that Combermere had expanded its curriculum and its sixth form offerings. He was especially pleased with the expansion that had taken place in the science department, as he was convinced that nobody could make much progress in this century without some training in the general sciences.[72]

After functioning for two years at Waterford, Combermere was carefully inspected by a team of experts led by Stanley Moffett, the director of education. The inspectors thought that the school should be commended for the manner in which it had so heroically weathered so many storms since 1943. They also felt that it should be given more time to settle down in its new environment. Their overall recommendations included more emphasis on the training of teachers, greater economy in the school's staffing, streaming of students at eleven-plus, the abolition of the preparatory form, restriction of the sixth form to students of real merit, the gradual abandonment of commercial subjects, and the rehabilitation of the school library.[73]

The Combermere staff rejected the majority of these recommendations at once. They disagreed with the idea of streaming students at eleven-plus and argued for the retention of the prep. They vehemently denied that the school was too liberally staffed, and insisted on a ratio of 1:20 with fewer than thirty periods per week for each staff member. They called for the reintroduction of the compulsory stationery scheme, while using the opportunity also to draw attention to the lack of proper playing fields or proper boundaries.[74]

By the time of Noott's last Speech Day in 1961, the staff had grown to thirty-one, including twenty-six permanent members. Among them there were no fewer than twenty-one qualified teachers as the UCWI graduates, like Neilton Seale and Eustace Taitt, were now returning home. Thanks also largely to Noott's encouragement, Livy Goring and Charlie Best had completed their degrees externally. On the Combermere staff at this stage, too, was Calvin 'Archie' Yarde, who had come from the civil service with an external degree from London University. There were also a few non-graduates who had received professional training at Erdiston College, the local teacher training institution. Noott had thus remained at Combermere long enough to see his staff almost wholly qualified, as he had so fervently hoped from the very beginning.[75]

The most significant administrative change which occurred during Noott's last days as headmaster was the creation of the post of deputy headmaster, carrying considerable salary advantage and categorically defined rights and duties. The deputy was to be left in charge of examinations, timetables, discipline, education statistics and duty rosters.[76] The post of deputy is now a feature of all secondary schools in Barbados, but what is most significant here is that the duties laid down are much the same now as Noott had outlined for his second master in the 1940s. When the position was first advertised in 1957, Noott urged the governing body to appoint a teacher with academic distinction as well as administrative skills. Collymore was the obvious man for the post, for he was universally respected despite his lack of formal degrees, but he was only one year away from his official retirement.[77] As had happened just before Wilson's retirement in 1932, however, the staff again submitted a strong petition to the governing body championing the cause of Vincent Williams who had given the school thirty-eight years of faithful service and had already acted three times with great success as deputy headmaster, his lack of formal qualifications notwithstanding.[78]

Noott acceded to the request of his senior assistants and the governing body duly appointed Williams the deputy in April 1958.[79] This administrative development freed the headmaster from the performance of some of his previous assignments and permitted him to concentrate more fully on the general supervision of an expanding school which was far more difficult to administer in 1960 than it had been ten years before. Williams carried out his tasks quite satisfactorily and, in Noott's absence, supervised the move from the Garrison to Waterford at the end of August 1958 with quiet efficiency. Dennis Goddard acted as deputy in his place that year. But when Williams finally retired at the end of 1960, he was succeeded by Stanton Gittens as deputy.

Moving to Waterford

When Combermere entered Waterford, Noott tried to whip the new playing fields into usable shape as soon as he could, and the athletic life of the school was shortly resumed. But he never appeared to readjust comfortably to his new environment. For Weymouth, in effect his first permanent home since leaving Haverfordwest years ago, he had developed a profound and emotional attachment. While he had dedicated himself to beautifying that site,[80] he did not make the same conspicuous effort at Waterford. In fact, the Waterford phase of Noott's administration seemed, in many ways, anticlimactic. He himself looked prematurely jaded and few people were surprised when he sought early retirement at the age of fifty-five and returned to Britain in 1961.[81]

In evaluating Noott's performance, it is difficult to believe that he was headmaster of Combermere School for only fifteen years and that the bulk of his work was done only in the first ten. He embarked on a variety of ambitious projects and achieved a measure of success in most of them. He personally mapped out a strategy for the school in 1947 and there is hardly any aspect of its life that escaped his influence. That he was an excellent administrator there can be no question. He was also a good judge of character, and most of his appointees performed at a very high level of competence.

Regarding himself always as an administrator first and foremost, Noott taught only four periods per week until compelled by the Education Board to undertake a minimum of fifteen in 1954.[82] His perception of his task as headmaster was in keeping with the existing Scheme of Government for Combermere School (a copy of which had been sent to him on his appointment by the director of education in 1946). He insisted on his right to determine the school's texts and curriculum, to control methods of teaching and arrangement of classes and school hours, to supervise the work of all his assistants, to formulate the school's overall strategy, to maintain discipline with the general assistance of the deputy, and to ensure that teachers as well as pupils gave of their best at all times. In short, he considered himself to be ultimately responsible for the whole internal organization of Combermere. He was just as anxious to see his students perform well outside the classroom as within it. He was also very keen on the general maintenance of the grounds and buildings. In all of these attitudes and activities, Noott was exemplifying the major characteristics of effective principals as revealed in the more recent research literature.[83]

If Noott did not encourage the formation of a parent-teachers' association, he at least tried to meet the parents of every new boy at the start of the school year, and to chat with as many of them as possible at Speech Days and Sports Days. Indeed it is only in more recent years that the notion of parent-teacher associations has begun to catch on in Barbados. He gave great encouragement to the CSOBA, and tried to persuade some of the more prosperous alumni to donate scholarships to needy students. He also made valiant efforts to communicate with the larger community by his involvement in a variety of activities. He was very active in the *Alliance Française de la Barbade*, and helped in staging the Coronation Pageant in 1953. He was also a driving force behind the Marian Anderson concert which was staged at the Globe Theatre in 1954.[84]

In the bulk of Noott's endeavours, he had the full support of the school's governing body who seldom failed to accept his recommendations. On some occasions, he himself was quick to follow up proposals made by them, as was the case in 1949 when he acceded to C.A. Coppin's request and appointed Millington to introduce instrumental music to the school.[85] In general, they allowed him free rein to administer Combermere in accordance with the Scheme of Government (Resolution No.83/1945—Amendment to 12/1890) which had traditionally left the headmaster with considerable power and authority. Even though, in theory, Noott was competent only to make recommendations to the governing body with respect to appointments and other major decisions, the governing body seldom questioned his judgement. He was therefore allowed a much greater freedom of manoeuvre than is now possible under the Education Act of 1981. How Noott would have coped with the constraints now imposed on secondary school principals in Barbados is hard to say. It is almost impossible to imagine him working in a situation in which his powers and responsibilities were so severely limited.

A headmaster's worth can often be measured by examining the spontaneous reactions of pupils and parents. Major Noott was held in high esteem by the vast majority of Barbadians, who seemed genuinely saddened by his departure in 1961. Rev. E.J. Pierce, who thought that he had done wonders for Barbadian education, paid him an especially warm compliment in that year.[86] G.S.V. Petter, too, had commented favourably in 1956 on Noott's intelligence and foresight in broadening the intellectual horizons of the school.[87] Aubrey Douglas-Smith, the UCWI resident tutor, was moved to observe, after the Speech Day ceremony in 1956, that:

> *the story of Combermere in the last few years is something of an epic. Few Heads could have had greater difficulties to face: the fact that you have not merely endured them but have built this school into something with an unmistakable personality of its own shows not only great courage in you but also great originality.*[88]

Douglas-Smith regarded the comparison with Harrison College since 1952 as quite a fascinating story with the miracle climaxing with Combermere's triumphs in sport and music. The difference in Combermerians in 1956 and in 1949, when Douglas-Smith first arrived in Barbados, was most striking. He thought that the senior boys had greater poise and maturity despite the poverty in so many of their homes. Douglas-Smith congratulated Noott on these achievements while noticing also that he was most fortunate to have been assisted by such able staff members as Broodhagen, Collymore, Holder and Millington.[89] Douglas-Smith was speaking here for a

Major C.E. Noott and members of the CSOBA, 1946

majority of knowledgeable Barbadians. Major Noott had given the school a positive image, and as early as 1949 a "Lodge School Parent" had written to the editor of the *Barbados Advocate* praising Noott for his imaginative work at Combermere and wondering why the first-grade schools were so reluctant to follow his example.[90]

Major Noott was held in deep respect also by the majority of his former students. On a few occasions after his retirement he thus returned to a very warm welcome to the school. His humanity (which was often concealed beneath an aloof and commanding military presence) manifested itself from the beginning when he restricted corporal punishment to a few major offenses. He seldom punished boys before listening to their defence, and often gave them the benefit of the doubt when he thought that the teacher had been too unfair or severe. He also took a keen interest in the welfare of all, but particularly the brighter (but poorer) students and often found scholarships from the welfare fund which he himself had set up in 1947. Throughout his tenure of office, that fund proved to be a major source of salvation to many a bright but destitute pupil. It was indeed a vital necessity at a time when secondary education had not yet become free for Barbadian scholars. Most of the members of the first sixth form of 1952-53 were kept on at the school through Noott's generosity and interest. The files at Waterford contain many touching letters from former pupils who felt obliged to place on record their gratitude to him.[91]

To appreciate fully what Noott meant to a whole generation of Barbadians, the objective researcher has only to attend the meetings of the Combermere School Old Scholars' Association. These gatherings are invariably dominated by Noott's boys who sing his praises and recall examples of his charity and good humour. There are countless anecdotes which reflect Noott's humanity. Two will suffice here. A fourth former was once caught sleeping in his class. Noott's concern was not to punish the lad but to enquire about such matters as his diet, his workload at home, and the difficulties involved in his travelling to and from school. A senior boy was once reported by a master for writing impertinent lines. Noott listened to the defendant's case, read his "offensive" lines, complimented him on the quality of his English style and urged him to contribute to the school magazine.

It can be argued that Noott, like all of his predecessors, tried too hard to anglicize Combermere. He introduced British songs and British texts as well as British ideas and attitudes. But these were all he could have been expected to know. An individual, after all, must necessarily be the product of his or her training and environment. In any case, at that stage there was little Barbadian or West Indian material that Noott could possibly have utilized. Although his background was Welsh, he adopted Barbados as a second home. To the end of his life, Noott identified warmly with Combermere School and spoke glowingly of the days when his boys, Wes Hall, Patrick Lashley and Rawle Brancker, were members of the West Indies cricket team.

Noott was a remarkable person and head teacher. A man of vision and a disciplined man, he devoted himself to the development of Combermere and there is no doubt that his era was a turning point in its history. As A. Blumberg and W. Greenfield declared in 1980:

> *It takes a unique person to help give a school first, an image of what it can be and, second to provide the drive, support and skills to make that image approximate reality.*[92]

Noott was such a unique headmaster. He died in Wales, at eighty-five, on 7 February 1992. His death provided the occasion for a very moving memorial service which Old Combermerians dutifully held in the school hall. On 15 March 1993 the CSOSA, with the permission of the Ministry of Education and the Board of Management, named the school hall the Major Noott Hall and erected a plaque in the foyer to mark the occasion. The formal ceremony was doubly special because it was attended by Mrs Jacqueline Gregory, daughter of the major, her husband and their two children and the major's widow, Mrs Kathleen Noott, who unveiled the plaque.

The dynamism of Noott's Combermere was, in many ways, a reflection of the wider society in the immediate postwar period. The progressive forces unleashed by the Second World War left a positive impact on the entire British empire and Commonwealth. Traditional systems and programmes had to be reshaped or abandoned and even the conservative establishment in Barbados could no longer flout world opinion, to say nothing of public opinion at home. The colony began to press for ministerial government and to insist on a greater control over its own affairs. It could not therefore, in all conscience, deny the majority of its people the right to participate in the political process. Hence the gradual dismantling of the oligarchical structures that had left Barbados so long at the mercy of a small white élite.

The beginning of the end of the old order was marked by the extension of the franchise, first in 1943 and then in 1951, which totally transformed the complexion of the old electorate. Black voters promptly began to support black candidates and the House of Assembly, largely White when Noott first arrived in Barbados in 1946, was largely Black when he departed in 1961.[93] In much the same way, the ethnic composition of Noott's school witnessed a revolution. Noott found a sizeable contingent of white pupils at Combermere on his arrival. The number of white boys in attendance at the time of his departure could be counted on the fingers of a single hand.

It was during the age of Noott that the Barbados Labour Party (BLP) came to full maturity and its leader, G.H. (later Sir Grantley) Adams, thus served as the island's first premier. K.N.R. Husbands, another BLP member, became the first black Speaker of the House of Assembly. Ministerial government was introduced in 1954 and Barbados was an active member of the West Indian Federation which lasted from 1958 to 1962. One of its black leaders, Sir Grantley Adams, actually became its first (and only) prime minister. When the younger generation of black politicians became impatient with the more cautious approach recommended by Adams, they rejected his brand of leadership and founded the Democratic Labour Party (DLP) in 1955. Its first leader was Errol Walton Barrow, who became premier in 1961 and had the distinction of leading Barbados into independence in 1966.[94] It is unlikely that such vital changes could have occurred in Barbados and in the Caribbean without leaving some impact on Combermere's growth and development. These political developments led naturally to a mighty overhaul, at long last, of the old-fashioned fiscal system that had favoured the propertied classes at the expense of the majority. Barbados, as a consequence, found more money to spend on public causes, and it was during the age of Noott that the government began to devote considerably more dollars to such key areas as public health and education. Under the old system of taxation, Barbados could muster only £611,831 (about $2.94 million) in total revenues for 1939-40. Twenty years later, the island's receipts had risen to more than $23 million. Thus, while Combermere's government grant stood at £3,918 (approximately $18,800) for 1945-46, just before Noott arrived, it rose to $171,730 by 1959-60.[95] Noott was therefore able to effect more radical changes to his school than either Cox or Armstrong could ever have contemplated.

It is only fair to say, therefore, that Noott's Combermere profited enormously from the new climate of opinion. In 1947, when the Major was mapping out the first of his famous Five-year plans for the school, he was expected to make do with a government grant of $46,488. Within ten years, this amount had more than doubled.[96] What is even more significant, however, is the fact that the Combermere grants had become almost equal to those being offered to Harrison College and had already exceeded the amounts placed at the disposal of the Lodge School and Queen's College. The postwar legislature had begun its steady retreat from the traditional (and élitist) policy of treating the first-grade schools preferentially.

Chapter Five

CONSOLIDATION AT WATERFORD 1961-81

Major Noott had so thoroughly revitalized Combermere School that it would have been impossible for his immediate successors to undo his work. As it was, they consolidated it during the next twenty years. He was succeeded by Stanton Gittens, the younger brother of Lionel Gittens, who had taught at Combermere for twenty-one years before leaving in 1958 to take charge of the government printery in Bridgetown. Stanton and Lionel were the sons of an Old Combermerian, Lionel O. Gittens, a pianist and piano tuner, whose father had been a primary school teacher. They had thus sprung from a lower, but well-established, middle-class Barbadian family and Stanton was the first black native to be chosen to lead a secondary school of Combermere's size and importance.

Born on 4 May 1911, Gittens attended Combermere under Burton before winning a junior first-grade exhibition and joining his brother at Harrison College in 1924. He spent seven years at that school before studying for a classics degree at Codrington College. He then joined the Combermere staff under Armstrong in October 1934. After a stint of nine years, he left to take up an appointment at the Grenada Grammar School in January 1944. He spent but a single term there before returning to Barbados to serve as an assistant master at Harrison College. Thus, after an interval of almost eighteen years, Gittens rejoined the Combermere staff in 1961 when he was appointed deputy headmaster on Williams's retirement. He served as acting headmaster for one term while Noott was on pre-retirement leave, and then inherited the headship in 1961.[1]

Stanton came to Combermere with a reputation as a scholar/athlete in the 'Gussie' Cox tradition. He had been an excellent wicket-keeper, batsman and a competent soccer player in his younger days. For many years he had played cricket and soccer first for Combermere School and then Harrison College. He had also represented Barbados in eleven intercolonial cricket matches between 1935 and 1945, hitting a fine century against Trinidad in January 1937. He had made a valuable contribution to Combermere's memorable triumph in the BCA first division competition in 1940-41 before leading the Empire Cricket Club to a similar victory in 1941-42.[2]

Gittens found the school still trying to adjust to its new surroundings at Waterford. The staff left by Noott was largely young and inexperienced and still very unstable. This was a time when most teachers aimed at upgrading their qualifications since at long last the government had begun to pay much better salaries to attract graduates to the teaching profession. As a result, several non-graduates were constantly applying for study leave and temporary replacements had frequently to be sought. In fact, as Gittens morosely observed, Combermere had as many as thirteen acting appointees on its staff all at once in 1963. He also expressed some dismay over the reflection that not a single UCWI graduate had applied to fill any of the vacant posts at Combermere during his first three years as headmaster.[3]

By 1964, the Combermere staff had grown to thirty-four and included twenty-six graduates. Gittens had just managed to engage the services of Mr and Mrs Davies to teach English and French, Michael Owen to teach chemistry, and C.E. Aurelius Smith (who later became headmaster of the Lodge School) to teach physics. But staffing problems plagued the school throughout his tenure. As Gittens complained in 1964, timetabling was an extremely difficult matter because of the unusual fluidity of his nomadic staff.[4]

The staffing crisis reached a climax in the late 1960s with the opening of the new Community College which offered superior conditions of service to its teachers. No fewer than seven teachers resigned from Combermere on 31 December 1968, giving the governing body only minimal notice. Thus it was that Gittens had to seek immediate replacements for several teachers including Arthur Sealy, a senior Latin master, and C.W. Wickham, a senior Spanish teacher. Ralph Brathwaite, who had served Combermere so well as scoutmaster and manager of the bookstore, also retired in December 1968 after having taught at this school for more than twenty-four years. In March 1969, too, Combermere had to cope with the teachers' strike which disrupted the routine of most schools for several days. This teachers' strike took place as a result of a dispute over the significant differences in salaries and conditions of service between similarly qualified teachers who had recently been appointed to the staff of the Barbados Community College and their former colleagues in the older secondary schools. It was remarkable in that a few secondary school teachers challenged the ministry of education, and later on the government, in a spirit of principled defiance. Elsie (later Dame Elsie) Payne of Queen's College became the cogent and convincing spokesman for the teachers. Amidst dire threats, such as loss of jobs and pension rights by the prime minister, Errol Barrow, the teachers held firm and gained most of the ground over which the dispute had arisen. The governing body, following instructions from the government, decided to withhold salaries from those teachers who had not reported for duty during the strike and to pay only those who had shown a willingness to work.[5]

Previously the Barbados government had commissioned an enquiry into the working conditions of the island's teachers and civil servants. The Jacobs Commission of 1961 emphasized the need to upgrade teachers' salaries in Barbados, to bridge the gap between the teaching and civil services and to remove the disparity between the sexes. It recommended that women should be brought gradually into line with men by a series of instalments, and advocated additional allowances for the supervision of games, libraries and departments as well as administrative posts within the schools.[6] As these recommendations began to take effect, the staffing situation improved, only to run into the crises of 1968-69. Thereafter, however, the Combermere staff gradually became more stable. In the middle and late 1960s Gittens appointed some thirteen graduate teachers, most of whom along with a small core of previously appointed staff remained to form the solid nucleus of the Moore staff during the 1970s.[7]

It was this hard core of assistants who helped Gittens see Combermere through its early Waterford transition. The various programmes introduced in the late 1950s took root during the Gittens period. The science programme, for instance, steadily expanded and the headmaster was able to report that the new science block would be officially opened in September 1964. Whereas only fifty students had taken science subjects at Waterford in 1958, the number had risen to 500 within six years.[8] Combermere also managed to develop its industrial arts programme. The industrial arts wing was completed in February 1963 and teaching in woodwork and metalwork was begun during the Trinity term the same year.[9]

During the 1960s, the school library was rehabilitated at last. The rebuilding process had actually begun with the appointment of 'Charlie' Best as school librarian in Noott's later days. However, he left in 1961 to accept a teaching position in the Turks and Caicos Islands (before returning to Barbados to head the Community College later on). The building originally intended to serve as the headmaster's residence was soon found inappropriate for that purpose and was converted into the school library in 1963.[10] This not only provided more classroom space but also allowed the school to extend its library holdings. In 1970, the library increased its stock of books by purchasing Livy Goring's private collection for $800, paid in two instalments. Goring sold his collection when he was about to take up his appointment as consul general for Barbados in New York.[11]

The musical tradition which Noott had established was kept alive. After James Millington retired from the permanent staff, Gittens appointed Dr John Fletcher, an accomplished pianist, whom he described as perhaps "the most highly qualified musician in the Caribbean area".[12] Fletcher came in January 1964 and remained on the Combermere staff until his retirement in 1991. In the early 1960s, too, Gerald Hudson retired after having been the school's visiting music instructor for twenty-seven years (1935-62). During the Gittens period, even when other examination results were disappointing, the musicians consistently performed very well.[13] The headmaster was sufficiently encouraged by their work to seek an expansion of the Combermere instrumental music programme in 1969. He therefore acquired two flutes, one oboe, four clarinets, three trumpets and two tenor trombones. Faced with a shortage of instrumental music tutors Gittens requested help from the Royal Barbados Police Band.[14] Gittens's abiding interest in instrumental music sprang from his background and training. His own father had remained a popular Barbadian musician for many years.

Under Gittens, Combermere did well also in the field of sports, which is not surprising—considering that the headmaster continued to take an extremely keen interest in athletic activity. It won the prestigious Dalton Cup for soccer for the first time in 1963 and was victorious that year too in the Ronald Tree Cup competition in cricket. The extracurricular activities of the school expanded to include basketball and table tennis which had not been much played by Combermerians previously.[15] The Combermere School Cadet Company and the Combermere School Scout Troop remained very active during this decade, and the headmaster's profound interest in the welfare of these two movements is reflected in the fact that he left to posterity fuller records pertaining to them than to any other features of the school's life.

Gittens attempted to revive the school magazine but succeeded only in producing a single issue. Too many copies were printed by the school and only a few of them could be sold. It proved to be a very costly venture therefore and was not repeated in Gittens's time. In fact, among the school's records at Waterford, there are still hundreds of unsold copies of the *Combermere School Magazine* for December 1964. But, like Burton and Noott before him, Gittens recognized the value of a school magazine and the need to keep the students involved in its production. He wanted it to serve, as much as anything else, as the pupils' mouthpiece. Hence the magazine committee which he struck in 1963 included six senior boys and only two masters, E.B. Davies and C.W. Pilgrim.

Gittens inherited a school of approximately 650 pupils and a staff of thirty. He saw it grow to a roll of about 780 students and forty-four teachers in just over nine years.[16] The staff by 1970 had

The staff, 1967–68, including S.O'C. Gittens, C.DeV. Moore, C.W. Pilgrim and K.A. Roach who have administered Combermere since 1961

become more seasoned and stable and had a great deal to do with the success which the school achieved in the 1960s. Vere Moore emerged as the deputy early in the decade and ensured a certain measure of continuity. Pilgrim, another veteran, continued to make a vital contribution and was especially responsible for the resurrection of the Literary and Debating Society which was one of the very few institutions which Noott had permitted to languish during the 1950s. Harry Sealy, who had succeeded Lionel Gittens as master in charge of the junior school in 1958, continued to serve in that capacity until his own retirement in 1980. He was the only surviving Armstrong appointee and was destined to teach at Combermere for over forty years, including the period from 1980 to 1983 when he returned as an acting assistant master.

Assessing the Role of Stanton Gittens

It is extremely difficult to reach a verdict on Gittens's role in and contribution to Combermere's evolution. He was not an able administrator in the mould of a Major Noott. Nor was he considered to be a particularly good teacher. In fact, he was described as an abrasive man, reportedly not a little disliked by the majority of his colleagues as well as his pupils. To the teaching/learning situation and to discipline he unfortunately brought a brusque and militaristic approach, in which the questionable practice of corporal punishment, whose dubious virtues he stressed, featured prominently. Even though corporal punishment was not the norm at Combermere before the Gittens regime, it must be pointed out that this form of punishment was still very prevalent in the country at the time. Caution, therefore, has to be exercised against invoking today's attitudes and standards in any assessment of Gittens's practices. Be that as it may, however, he clearly believed that almost any problem within the school could be solved by the application of a caning. At the end of each term, for example, he would routinely flog large numbers of students who had, in his judgement, performed below their full potential. The full effect of caning is always difficult to assess. Does it deter? Does it bring about improved performance or behaviour? Or does it exacerbate bad attitudes and bad behaviour? What appears quite clearly in this instance is that it contributed tremendously to Gittens's unpopularity.

Gittens was, from all accounts, the most unpopular headmaster in the history of Combermere School. The vast majority of his former colleagues are convinced that the school's continued growth was due to unexplained factors quite unrelated to him or his administrative leadership, or interpersonal relationships skills. That the staff continued to carry on functioning satisfactorily as a unit was very much due to the qualities of C. DeV. Moore, the deputy headmaster, who served as a buffer between Gittens and his colleagues. This assessment seems somewhat facile and convenient. The school continued to enjoy a measure of success on too many fronts to support such a dismissive stance. Indeed, later events would show that C. DeV. Moore was not himself, a resounding success in his own right as headmaster. Gittens, after all, did not leave the school on automatic pilot while he relaxed. He sought to convey a clear message about the value of hard work and application to his students, even if he used what both they and his colleagues considered the wrong medium. If he did not introduce any significant innovation, he at least nurtured and consolidated much that had only recently been instituted. He took useful initiatives, for example, in music, staffing and in extracurricular activities and he had to weather a few storms. Furthermore, while in assessing the work of headmasters, significant attention is placed on what they do, one must not overlook the importance of what they permit others to do.

Nevertheless, when Gittens departed in December 1970, there was no overflowing of emotion as was witnessed in 1925 or 1961 or as would be seen again in 1986. If anything at all, there was a feeling of relief when he left. He bequeathed to posterity no articulate statement or philosophy that can now be used to dissect his methodology or to help the researcher understand the motivating impulses behind his administrative decisions. Whereas even the casual and easygoing Armstrong had left numerous documents, Gittens left practically nothing. One searches in vain among the voluminous records at Waterford for letters or memoranda from this administrator. Apart from his cadet file and examination registers, there is not a great deal of recorded data on the period of his headship.

The historian is therefore left entirely at the mercy of oral testimony. Many of Gittens's former students find it difficult to explain his unswerving devotion to corporal punishment. Some of his former colleagues dismiss him simply as an old-fashioned martinet, lacking in sensitivity and civility. A few of his younger assistants recall that he showed no particular interest in their welfare or progress. If, therefore, we appear to quote too liberally from three of Gittens's former students, it is to provide a view of that seldom seen side of him. There is first, the testimony of Phil Branch, an Old Combermerian, who is now a senior assistant master at the Lodge School. Fresh from the sixth form, Branch had joined the Combermere staff in 1956. He applied for study leave in 1963 to pursue an honours degree in geography at the University of Toronto. Gittens gave this application his full support even though the governing body's reaction to it was mixed, to say the least. In the end Branch went off to Toronto with a government scholarship as well as financial assistance from Combermere School. He was allowed one year's leave on full pay and two years on half. Gittens was determined to help Branch upgrade his qualifications and his skills in the hope of tying a promising young geographer to the Combermere staff on a permanent basis.[17]

There is also the testimony, even more eloquent, of two of Gittens's very successful students: Ronald Ainsley Bruce, a highly successful chartered accountant with Saskpower in Regina, and Dr Keith Albert Sandiford, a professor of English at Louisiana State University. Both are convinced that Gittens has been too negatively portrayed by their contemporaries. They insist that the continuing growth in the number of graduate teachers in the 1960s was by no means an accident. They see it as due in no small part to the headmaster's personal dedication to improving the professional quality of his staff. They view the recruitment of Dr John Fletcher, for instance, as a singular stroke of forward thinking no less dramatic than Noott's appointment of Millington some fifteen years before. Nor, in their opinion, was the extension of science teaching at the school merely fortuitous. It was Gittens who deliberately tried to ensure that a larger percentage of the total pupil body received some training in these disciplines. Such innovations as maths sets—the idea of teaching maths by ability groups—could not have succeeded without his approval and support, even if it can be argued that this particular notion originated with Ben Browne, the senior mathematics teacher. If Noott deserves credit for the A level results in 1953, when eight of ten certificates were achieved in French and history, then surely Gittens should likewise be applauded for the quality of the O level results in 1963, which were among the best in the school's history of writing Oxford and Cambridge examinations. The objection here, of course, is that the 1953 results were achieved by students whom Noott had admitted to the school in 1947 and those in 1963 were accomplished by boys who had also largely been trained during the years of Noott's administration. Gittens's supporters are on firmer ground, however, when they argue that he should be commended for producing the school's first Barbados Scholar (Shepherd) in 1967.

Bruce and Sandiford agree that Gittens, like Burton and Noott, accorded sixth formers and prefects diverse opportunities to develop their leadership capacities. He extended the prefect corps, as Noott had done, to ensure a more meaningful ratio of officers to the rank and file. He supported them in the exercise of their duties and emphasized to the rest of the school that the prefects' authority flowed directly from the headmaster's and could not therefore be flouted with impunity. His attitude to the staff was the same. He gave his assistant masters unwavering support both within and outside the classroom and never allowed the pupils to question or to undermine their authority in any way. The full value of this approach came to be much appreciated later on when, to the dismay of the teachers and prefects alike, his successor permitted too many offenders to escape scot free. Many of Gittens's boys, however, are still bitter about his blunt refusal to listen to their defence when unfairly charged by masters or prefects, and some of the masters themselves are still convinced that he was too willing to find an excuse for resorting to corporal punishment.

In the opinion of his supporters, Gittens also tried to expand the mental horizons of his senior students by providing special periods for scholarship teaching. He often invited Rev. Genders and Rev. Layne from Codrington College to discuss questions of ethics, and scheduled some special lectures on current affairs by selected members of staff. He constantly exhorted his sixth formers to sustained application for scholarly attainment, and even insisted that athletes should not represent the school unless they maintained passing standards in the classroom.

In testifying on Gittens's behalf, Sandiford (who was both a student and a teacher at the school in Stanton's time) wrote to one of the authors a long and excellent letter on the topic, the last paragraph of which deserves to be quoted in full:

> *Under Gittens, Combermere finally claimed its right to full citizenship in the community of leading secondary schools. If the Sixth Form sets the tone and pattern of a school's ethos, I would say that the Combermere generation which grew into maturity under Gittens evinced a marked sense of self-confidence about who they were as Combermerians; my colleagues felt themselves the equal of any Harrison College or Lodge boy, and on the whole both their exam results at Combermere and their subsequent achievements farther afield vindicate that feeling. They caught the sparks*

of pride bequeathed them by preceding generations and kept vigorously alight that flame which the school song has taught us to look to as our moral emblem. They took with them into the world an understated self-consciousness about the growing stature of their school which quickened the respect of an ever watchful public.[18]

This is Professor Sandiford's considered verdict which agrees in all of its essentials with Ron Bruce's testimony. They sincerely believe that Gittens made a vital contribution to Combermere's development, notwithstanding his shortcomings. In response to the remark about equality with other secondary schools, however, it can readily be noted that the distinction between first-grade and second-grade secondary institutions in Barbados had, in fact, been removed by the DLP government in the very first year of Gittens's tenure. There was therefore no need for Sandiford's generation of Combermerians to feel in any way inferior to Harrisonians. Indeed we are not aware of any generation of Combermerians feeling inferior in any way to Harrisonians or anybody else.

As the first black headmaster of an important school, Gittens was saddled with an onerous responsibility. He was also faced with the challenge of succeeding a Welsh headmaster who had left a truly enviable reputation and he must have felt that he was walking constantly in Noott's ample shadow. He seemed to think he had a trust to preserve and this must have weighed heavily upon him. The task of keeping up grounds and physical plant with only a very small maintenance staff must have made that task particularly trying. He somehow seemed to fear that the school would collapse before his very eyes, and it is probably important to stress that this fear was not altogether unfounded. Combermere is located at the hub of several densely populated communities, such as Bush Hall, Green Hill, Spooner's Hill and Waterford. Gittens's challenge was to pursue the ethos of the school while permitting its influence to reach out and modify the behaviour of the working-class environment in which the school was situated. Combermere has always reached beyond the confines of its walls into the village and shared its goals and its facilities with the villagers.

Vere Moore as Headmaster

Gittens was succeeded by Moore who had served as his deputy and had been associated with Combermere since 1946. Born on 9 October 1921, Cuthbert de Vere 'Bumpy' Moore was the son of an elementary school headmaster, and came from a social and academic background very similar to that of the Gittens brothers. He was an Old Harrisonian who had studied also at Codrington College and Durham University before emerging in the mid-1950s with a B.A. and a Dip. Ed. In 1953, he had unsuccessfully sought an extension of his study leave from Combermere and had resigned his original appointment.[19] He resumed teaching at the school, however, when he returned to Barbados in 1955 after an absence of five years. With the departure of almost all the Armstrong appointees, Moore had suddenly become the most senior graduate on the permanent staff during Noott's final year.[20]

Endowed with a wry sense of humour, Vere Moore was a quiet, soft-spoken individual, who had been a perfect foil to the more aggressive Gittens in the 1960s. Many of his colleagues, however, considered him insufficiently dynamic to assume a position of authority. The Board of Education, apparently agreeing with them, did not appoint him to the headship until 1972 after he had served several terms as the acting headmaster.[21]

By 1972, the school had grown to almost 800, but it was now administered by a relatively mature staff. Apart from Charles Pilgrim, who was soon named deputy headmaster in place of Aurelius Smith who was appointed headmaster of the Lodge, Moore's colleagues included several who had taught at the school for some years under Gittens. Some of them, indeed, such as Blyden Callender, Douglas Campbell, Keith King and Cedric Phillips, had also had considerable teaching experience before coming to Combermere.[22]

In many ways, Moore was unlike any previous Combermere headmaster. He was not a scholar/athlete like Armstrong, Cox or Gittens; nor was he a military leader like Noott; and neither was he a distinguished teacher like Burton. His main quality was his profound humanity. Deeply hating to offend, he was perpetually anxious to please. As a result, he often had great difficulty reaching positive decisions and his tendency was to wait out a crisis, doing nothing in the hope that the problem would shortly solve itself. This simple strategy after a while exasperated his colleagues, who came more and more to look for effective leadership from the deputy headmaster. The period of Moore's administration therefore is, in a sense, the beginning of the Pilgrim regime.

Moore did not have the strength of will to revolutionize Combermere. His school remained in essence the same institution that he had inherited. The 1970s witnessed continuing expansion of the student population and the roll gradually reached 843 by 1978. The staff had to be increased to cope with these additional pupils and had risen to 52 by the end of the decade. The salaries, too, had continued to explode to the point where there could be no meaningful comparison between the school's budgets prepared by Noott and those that Moore had to contemplate. In September 1946, for example, when the Major signed his first monthly paysheet, the total bill for his teachers' salaries came to $2,531. During that year, 1946-47, the Department of Education allotted £7,462 (i.e. $35,817) of its total revenues (£196,987) to Combermere. In Noott's final year, 1960-61, the bill for his teaching staff came to more than $140,000 in an overall budget of about $181,000. His own salary, over a period of fifteen years had risen from $3,600 to $7,920. The dramatic escalation of salaries and prices during the 1960s and 1970s forced the Combermere annual budget beyond half a million dollars in the early 1970s and it reached $1.3 million in Moore's final year, when his own salary rose to $30,000—having almost doubled during his tenure of the headship.[23]

But while there was continuing expansion of staff, student body and school budgets, there were no dramatic shifts in direction or curriculum. The one remarkable development which made the age of Moore quite different from its predecessors was the decision, reached by him in 1976 without prior consultation with his colleagues, to agree with the ministry of education to make Combermere a coeducational school. Thus, almost overnight, the school had to rearrange its methods and strategies to cope with the introduction of girls. For some time previously, there had been a trickle of female sixth formers into Combermere, but after 1976 that trickle became a steady stream. Between 1972 and 1976, the school had admitted a carefully chosen handful of senior girls to study A level subjects, and they had generally served as a source of inspiration to the senior boys.

By increasing the number of girls annually, the ratio of males to females was almost 1:1 by 1982.[24] By this time, the school had readjusted. When the girls first arrived, however, Moore had made no provision for their recreational activities or even their lavatories, and there were no curricular or instructional adjustments. It was therefore an unhappy transition, as the girls felt unwanted and some of the more conservative boys and teachers did little to make them feel at home. In the end, however, the girls became accepted and are now an indispensable element within the school, participating actively in most features of Combermerian life.[25] They have added a new dimension even to the school's cadet company. Although his colleagues regretted the manner in which Moore had transformed Combermere into a coeducational institution, they later agreed that the decision was a good one and the Combermere tradition has been much enriched by it. The advent of coeducation was accompanied by the move to appoint more female teachers. Thus, by 1978, there were as many as sixteen women on the Combermere staff and the number rose to eighteen, in a total of fifty-one, during 1982-83.[26] This too was a significant departure from tradition. Apart from Gloria Escoffery, who had occasionally assisted Broodhagen in the teaching of art and Mrs Gloria Blackman who was on staff in the late 1950s, Combermere had known no female instructors during the age of Noott.

It was during Moore's time, too, that the Combermere School Old Boys Association was suddenly revived in 1973 by Ezra Alleyne, George Belgrave, Wendell McLean, Glynne Murray and others.[27] It had initially replaced the Combermere Mutual Improvement Association in 1934 and had generally prospered during the period of Armstrong and Noott. As late as 1963, it had established the Armstrong Memorial Prize as a tribute to the former headmaster who, at the age of eighty-two, had just died on his way back from England to Barbados. Inexplicably, however, it had become almost defunct in the late 1960s, even though the U.S. branch of the association had held a celebration at the school to mark its 150th anniversary in 1969.[28] In 1977, acknowledging the school's coeducational status, the CSOBA gave way to the Combermere School Old Scholars' Association which has developed into one of the most dynamic of all such groups of alumni in Barbados during the past decade.[29]

In the history of Combermere School, the Gittens and Moore periods possess a certain sense of dramatic unity. All the elements of the Noott tradition were kept in place. The sixth form became the pride of the school and won a few scholarships and exhibitions. The introduction of the Common Entrance Examinations in 1959 and the abolition of tuition fees after 1961 completed superficially, at least, the removal of the old distinctions between first-grade and second-grade secondary schools. Gittens and Moore lost some of their freedom with respect to admissions but that did not seem to matter a great deal at that time. The cadet company prospered under such able leaders as Deighton Maynard and Patrick Skeete, and the Combermere School Scout Troop remained alive after celebrating its fiftieth anniversary in 1962.[30] A new and important feature, however, was the growth of the Combermere School Cadet Band during the 1970s. It gave the school's image a substantial boost by performing so well and so frequently in parades and other public functions.[31]

On the field of play, Combermere continued to do well in its spacious playgrounds, dominating the school field hockey competition throughout the Gittens and Moore periods. In 1973-74, it played unbeaten in the interschool competition for the sixth consecutive year.[32] In that sport, it produced two fine international stars in Ralph Holder and Harcourt Wason. The latter represented Barbados for many years afterwards. Combermere also played consistently good soccer, doing extremely well in two divisions during the early 1970s when it boasted the promising Peter Alkins who was eventually selected to represent Barbados.[33] The cricket teams also did the school proud occasionally, as was the case when the Ronald Tree Cup was won in 1976.[34] On the track, the school produced the versatile Wason, one of the island's greatest quarter-milers, who often represented Barbados in international competition. While still at school, he won silver medals for Barbados at the Carifta Games in 1973. He was, in fact, the outstanding

Combermerian athlete of the 1970s. He ultimately returned to the school as its physical education specialist to carry on the great tradition established by Harold Brewster and Bruce St John.[35] Wason is still heavily involved in the coaching and management of Barbadian track teams both at home and abroad.

The Gittens and Moore periods also witnessed an overhauling of the house and prefect system. In 1964, to cope with the increasing number of students, the prefect corps was increased to fifty. Each set was now to have eight officers, including a captain, vice-captain, three prefects and three sub-prefects. The sub-prefects were to retire at the end of each school year and then be eligible for re-election. Only fifth and sixth formers were eligible for the office of full prefect, captain or vice-captain. Fourth formers could be elected sub-prefects. The right of nominating candidates for election to office rested with a committee comprising the headmaster, his deputy, the house masters, the games masters, and such members of staff as taught in the upper school. The prefects were to consider themselves perpetually on duty and to set a good example to the rest of the school.[36] This Prefects' Charter was revised again in 1971 allowing each set a house representative who was usually one of the senior prefects. Set F, formerly known as Weymouth House, was now officially changed to Worrell House as a tribute to that great Combermerian cricketer who had died prematurely in 1967, after having been knighted for his services to the game. One of the more negative results of these reforms was that the students lost some of the democratic rights that they had previously been allowed under Major Noott.[37]

Introduction of Departmental Heads

To cope with continuing expansion, the ministry of education overhauled the administration of the secondary schools. In addition to the deputy headmaster, seven formal departmental headships were created at Combermere in 1970. These heads of department were a source of considerable support to the beleaguered headmaster and were especially useful in determining timetables and curricula and coordinating programmes within their specialty. The earliest heads of these departments were A.L. Barrett (chemistry), Keith Roach (English), Jean Jordan (foreign languages), Dorien Pile (geography), Charles Pilgrim (history), Clarrie Layne (mathematics), and Lola Larrier (physics). By 1976-77, they were being paid $600 each per annum to run their separate departments.[38] Towards the end of Moore's tenure, John N. Payne (foreign languages), Janice Mayers (history), and Ben Browne (mathematics) joined the ranks of departmental heads replacing the earlier appointees who had moved on.

It was these departmental heads who provided detailed examination reports after 1977 to permit a more careful analysis than is possible for earlier periods. The results were often chequered with the school performing much better in English, history and music than in the foreign languages and the sciences. The physics results were especially bad during 1975-78, but showed considerable improvement in 1979. Mrs Larrier consistently blamed these disastrous results on the crippling instability of her staff. Barrett complained in 1977 that science was still an unpopular option and too few students were prepared to make the necessary effort. In 1979, he complained about the difficulties created by the lack of a biology laboratory which had been promised for more than seven years and which, one year later, was still missing. Payne often bemoaned the apathy on the part of the pupils, but thought in 1980 that the introduction of the tough Caribbean Examination Council (CXC) papers in Spanish had provided additional problems both for them and the staff. Browne felt that the absence of a mathematics room, which his department had been requesting since 1972, had much to do with the generally mediocre results in his discipline. He too considered the CXC papers too demanding. The English literature results were always worse than those achieved in English language and the difference between the two fields became even more noticeable when the school changed over to the CXC examinations in 1980. Miss Mayers thought that the history results at the O level were very good between 1975 and 1980 though the A levels were disappointing. She had just cause, however, to rejoice in 1980 when two of her students reached exhibition standard and one achieved a distinction for the first time in five years.[39]

The examination reports reveal that too much equipment was still lacking at Waterford even as late as 1980. The students were severely handicapped by the absence, for instance, of a biology laboratory which meant that their practical results were continually bad. The failure to secure a suitable teacher also had disastrous consequences for physics; and the transition from Oxford and Cambridge to CXC papers caused considerable difficulty—especially in mathematics and Spanish, where the examiners seemed to place unrealistic demands on their candidates.[40] But one of the most interesting features of these reports is the absence of any attempt, on the part of the departmental heads, to examine the standard of teacher preparation and quality of teaching.

It is difficult to estimate Moore's impact on these examination results. He was not a strong enough personality to have imprinted his stamp upon them or indeed on too many of the school's activities. On the other hand, his staff had become extremely well qualified and the departmental heads were quite experienced. By 1977-78, there were forty-six full-time members of Moore's staff and only two of them were non-graduates. Many of them, in fact, held more than one degree.[41] It is possible therefore to argue that the headmaster assumed they could be left to run their respective departments without any supervision from him and with no system of accountability except an analysis of examination results after the event.

Eventually Moore retired in 1981. He left Combermere in July, went on pre-retirement leave, and died on 18 December that same year at the age of sixty.[42] 'Bumpy' was well-liked by the boys even though most of them now agree that he was perhaps too lenient in his treatment of misconduct and misdemeanour. He was also well-liked by his colleagues although they were often frustrated by his notorious lack of resolution. He was deeply and universally mourned at his death, and the C. DeV. Moore Memorial Garden in the school's inner quadrangle was restored and dedicated, four years later, as a lasting tribute to him.[43] Combermere did not much suffer from the headship of Moore or that of Gittens. The school routine had been too well established and the tradition which had carefully been nourished from Speed to Noott could not easily be destroyed in two short decades. The period from 1961 to 1981 was essentially one of consolidation. It was the time when most of the seeds planted by Major Noott finally brought forth good fruit.

Once again the school's history and development mirrored the environment in which Gittens and Moore operated. During these twenty years, the wider community itself witnessed consolidation. Ministerial government had given way to independence, and Barbadian politics came to be dominated by the BLP and the DLP, both led by Blacks with almost identical backgrounds and philosophies. The earlier work done by such progressive politicians as Sir Grantley Adams, Mencea Cox, Wynter Crawford, Hugh Springer and Frank Walcott was continued by J.M.G.M. 'Tom' Adams, Errol Barrow, Bernard St John, Erskine Sandiford and Cameron Tudor. Both parties, while in power, continued the policy of remedial reforms which significantly improved the quality of life for most Barbadians.

A community, which had been able to collect only $26 million in total revenues during Stanton Gittens's first year as headmaster of Combermere, could boast receipts in excess of $450 million by the time of Vere Moore's death. The island allocated $4.5 million to education during 1961-62. Its education budget for 1980-81 exceeded $90 million.[44] This kind of growth allowed the country to increase by leaps and bounds the salaries of all teachers and public servants and gave considerable encouragement to young scholars and bureaucrats to upgrade their skills and qualifications. As a result, the teaching staffs of most schools in Barbados became more highly skilled so that these developments at the Gittens-Moore Combermere were not unusual in this respect. If Combermere witnessed a steady influx of new students, so too did all the other secondary schools as the DLP government had introduced a system of free secondary education in the 1960s and begun to build other secondary schools in response to popular demand.

Chapter Six

COMBERMERE SCHOOL SINCE 1981

During the 1970s, especially in Moore's later years, Combermere had become accustomed to being led, *de facto*, by Charles Pilgrim, the deputy headmaster. He took charge of the school on those occasions when Moore had decided to respond to a problem by pretending that it had disappeared. Born on 12 September 1930 into a socioeconomic background very similar to that of Gittens and Moore, Pilgrim was an Old Harrisonian who had been editor of his school's magazine in 1949-50, his last year there.[1] He went off immediately to study English and history at the UCWI at Mona and returned to take up an acting position on the Combermere staff in September 1953. He was appointed to a permanent post on 1 September 1955 and was therefore one of the longest serving members of the staff when selected in 1972 by the governing body to assume the responsibilities of deputy headmaster, and he was generally regarded as the natural successor to Moore when the latter retired in 1981.

Pilgrim was determined to provide Combermere School with more aggressive and effective administration than it had had since Noott's departure in 1961. He was a staunch admirer of Major Noott and set out to re-establish some of the businesslike, if not military, attitudes on which Noott had insisted. As early as 1977, when serving as the acting headmaster, he had expressed displeasure at some of his colleagues' indiscretions: leaving forms unattended, being absent without letter or notice, and lateness, among other things. He called for more rigid discipline both from the masters and the boys in Moore's absence.[2]

This approach he maintained when chosen headmaster during the 1981-82 academic session. Even the students discerned a marked change in the school's leadership and expected the new headmaster to be stricter than his predecessor and they did not resent it. In fact, there was a transparent mood of optimism when Pilgrim took over, as most of the staff members felt that Combermere had somehow been adrift but was now on the threshold of a renaissance. This positive mood was not immediately translated into improved examination results but it was undeniably there nevertheless.

Pilgrim was a fine teacher of English and history, had shown an interest in the cadets in his earlier days, and was a driving force behind such extracurricular movements as the Literary and Debating Society and the Photographic Club. He was an immensely popular member of the staff and had no difficulty establishing a good rapport with both pupils and colleagues. His easy, down-to-earth, no-nonsense approach appealed to many. He was therefore able to receive wholehearted support from the governing body and its successor, the board of management, during his brief stint.

'Charlie', as he was known to all, made it obvious that he intended the school to function smoothly even though he had no wish to behave in the manner of a martinet. He wanted to find a happy medium between the excessive severity of Gittens and the frustrating inertia of Moore. The students responded positively to this kind of approach, especially those in the upper forms whom he always treated as adults. It is clear that he would have taken the school beyond the horizons which Noott had envisaged had he not been discouraged by the unforeseen developments of the 1980s.

The Age of Pilgrim coincided with the introduction of the Education Act (1981) that replaced the governing bodies of the former grammar schools with new boards of management with lesser powers and restricted the authority of headmasters in some areas. There appeared to be a greater emphasis on red tape than had previously been the case and this caused the new Combermere headmaster considerable concern. He was far more interested in getting things done than in obeying formal rules and procedures. His kind of personality does not react well to the constraints implicit in the new Education Act which completed the inexorable process of centralization which had begun in the 1890s. As more and more aspects of the school's life fell under the supervision of the ministry of education, some of the headmasters in the older grammar schools felt that they were being emasculated. Pilgrim lost his faith in the system altogether when he was sued by the ministry of education in 1983 for having overstepped the legal bounds of his authority in the matter of admissions to the school. Like Hugh Barker of the Foundation School, he won his case, but seemed to lose some interest in Barbadian education. He retired from the headship of Combermere after five short years.[3]

The zest with which Pilgrim accepted the initial challenge in 1981 was so infectious that it permeated the entire school. The Literary and Debating Society, for instance, became far more active than it had been previously. The cadets, scouts and sporting teams performed with more than their usual verve, and the subcommittees established by the new board of management in 1983 were able to submit uniformly favourable reports about Combermere's life and work.[4] Even the CSOSA became conspicuously more vigorous in the 1980s than at any time before. Pilgrim also encouraged the growth of the Parent Teachers' Association to ensure greater communication between his assistants and the wider community.

The introduction of the Common Entrance Examination in 1959 had meant that the brightest eleven-year-old pupils had the right to attend the secondary school of their choice. For many years, Harrison College and the Lodge School had been the leading choices for boys and Queen's College for girls. But beginning at the time of Pilgrim's headship, the public image of the school was much improved and it gradually became a force to be reckoned with, with respect to choices at the Common Entrance Examinations. Combermere's examination results after 1982 were also much better than those of the 1970s, culminating in three Barbados Scholarships and a number of exhibitions during the age of Pilgrim.[5]

During Moore's last year, the examination results had been disappointing. Even in history, in which Combermerians had traditionally performed quite well, only five of twelve candidates passed at A level and their highest passing grade was C. The results were so bad in industrial arts that Pilgrim had to convene an emergency meeting with E. Barrow, J. Mottley and R. Skinner, the three teachers in that field, in the hope of discovering some explanation for such a collapse. The meeting revealed an inexplicable shortage of texts while the teachers insisted that too many weak students were being shunted into the industrial arts stream simply on the basis of their manifest inability to do anything else. The only redeeming feature that year was the surprisingly good physics report – the best in many years – despite a leaky roof and countless termites which made the physics laboratory a frustrating place in which to work.[6]

But the examination results of 1982 were even more disastrous, due in no small part, the staff felt, to the governing body's decision to compel the staff to enter all fifth and sixth form candidates for the subjects they were studying, whatever the level of their preparedness. Only two of fourteen students passed history at A level, and no Combermerian in chemistry or biology scored a grade higher than E. In every department, it was claimed, the results revealed a definite need for more rigid screening at both levels and this was the crux of the teachers' petition when they met in protest with the governing body to discuss the tale of woe.[7] And yet no lack of screening could explain such bad results, especially in a school whose intake perform at a relatively high level on the Common Entrance Examination. It is interesting how teachers' assessments tend to focus mainly on students in matters of this kind. Situations like this emphasize the need for principals to establish proper systems for monitoring the work of teachers through their heads of department and adequate systems of communication to ensure that they are always kept abreast of what is going on so that appropriate staff development strategies and programmes can be put in place in good time. Surely the causes must have been far more fundamental and therefore deserving of deeper analysis and indeed, prior action. This situation was quite similar to the bitter criticisms made by the staff in 1959 when they objected to Noott's practice of automatic promotions and insisted on an alternative policy to the one he had pursued with similar consequences since 1947.[8] In both instances, the staff succeeded in making their point.

The immediate reintroduction of the screening process was followed, perhaps fortuitously, by markedly better results thereafter. The staff, in fact, had been supported by the ministry of education on this occasion. Mr Ralph Boyce, a senior education officer (now chief education officer) writing on behalf of the permanent secretary in the ministry of education, advised all head teachers that the government would not pay the examination fees for weaker students but would allow parents to enter doubtful candidates at their own expense and refund them in case of successful performance. The reports of 1983 made much better reading, except in foreign languages in which only two of ten passed A level French and none of the five who sat the A level Spanish. The English results were excellent, both in language and in literature, and twelve of sixteen science students passed biology and chemistry at A level. But all of these performances were dwarfed by the magnificence of David Jean-Marie, who was awarded a Barbados Scholarship, having achieved grades of A in mathematics, physics and chemistry. The upward trend continued in 1984 and 1985 before culminating in the outstanding results of 1987 when Combermere won more scholarships and exhibitions than in any previous year. The 1980s, on the whole, were a successful decade for the school. Apart from the performance of David Jean-Marie, exhibitions were won by Gary Slocombe in 1985, and Roderick Brathwaite and Irwin Gibson in 1987. Barbados Scholarships were achieved by Charles Boxill in 1986, Melanie Brathwaite in 1987, and Colin Depradine in 1988. Melanie had the unique distinction of becoming the first girl to win a Barbados Scholarship for Combermere School. Her examination papers were uniformly excellent.[9]

Effects of the Education Act of 1981

Despite these positive examination results, however, the main theme in the history of the school during the early 1980s was conflict. For most of that decade the staff and the board of management battled with the ministry of education over a wide range of issues. The chief bone of contention, in the beginning, was the headmaster's residence. When Moore retired in 1981, the governing body's advertisement of the vacancy drew sharp criticism from the ministry. Warning that the imminent Education Act would soon deprive the school of the right to appoint its own headmasters, the Ministry advised the governing body that it might perhaps be best to fill the vacancy after the implementation of the new bill.[10] The governing body ignored that warning on the ground that it was unreasonable to hold the school in suspense while the government was deciding how to implement a complicated and controversial statute that, in any case, was not yet binding. The governing body acted in accordance with current policy, appointed Pilgrim in Moore's place, and gave him the option of renting the headmaster's residence at 8% of his salary.[11] When Pilgrim accepted that offer in August 1982, Walter Burke, the permanent secretary in the ministry of education, sent the governing body an angry letter demanding compliance with the ministry's edict that the residence should be rented at 20% of the headmaster's salary if furnished and 15% if semi-furnished.[12] The unhappy correspondence continued until Pilgrim decided to remain in his own house, leaving the headmaster's residence at Waterford unoccupied and uncared for. That matter, in fact, had not yet been resolved when Pilgrim resigned from the headship in 1986.

The protracted bickering over the headmaster's residence was in keeping with other Combermerian developments after 1981. Most of the decisions reached by the governing body failed to meet with the approval of the minister of education. In 1982, for instance, the ministry refused to formalize and perpetuate the post of master in charge of the junior school which Noott had created in 1947. Sealy had fulfilled that responsibility most conscientiously after Lionel Gittens's resignation in 1958, but the ministry of education now ruled that the post had been personal to Sealy and would not be renewed after his retirement.[13] Sealy himself was then denied a renewal of his acting appointment on the staff in 1983. The governing body vainly protested the decision to abolish a vital administrative office that, in its view, had become even more crucial in 1982 than at the time of its creation.[14] Sealy had officially retired in 1980, at the age of sixty, after having given the school thirty-seven unbroken years of faithful service. He had returned in an acting capacity before the ministry of education emerged with the ruling that he was replaceable and there was therefore no need for Combermere to retain his services. Sealy, an ordinary teacher, was not, in the ministry's judgement, in the same category as Broodhagen, the artist, and Millington, the violinist. This verdict outraged the Combermere teachers who were also incensed by the ministry's refusal to grant them permission to hold a Professional Development Day in 1984.[15]

It must be said, in fairness to the ministry, that the creation of heads of department in the secondary schools had gone far towards solving many of the problems which had led Noott, in 1947, to create the administrative position which Gittens and Sealy had occupied with such distinction. By 1982, the need for a head of the junior school was perceived to be much less pressing. This view did not acknowledge the valuable work Sealy had always performed as a "guidance counsellor". He knew all his charges and was very approachable and empathetic. In a large secondary school, Sealy became "class teacher" to the former elementary pupils. Hindsight has shown the value of this in preventing alienation and allowing for the easy integration of the new pupils into the school each year. Furthermore, while the newer secondary schools now had both heads of department responsible for academic matters related to their particular departments and senior teachers or year heads with responsibility for discipline, care and administrative matters with respect to each year group, no provision was made, until much later, for the latter posts in the older grammar schools.

One of the purposes of the Education Act (1981), was to remove the differences between the newer secondary schools which were less academic in orientation and the traditional grammar schools. They were now all officially termed secondary schools but some of the actual differences were only gradually removed. Others are far too deep-seated to be affected by a mere change in nomenclature. However, the decision to refuse acting positions to retired teachers was also reasonable. The ministry of education was not isolating Sealy for special mistreatment. Its ruling against him was in keeping with a general policy made urgent by the abundance of young university graduates then available.

In all of these hassles, nevertheless, Pilgrim and his staff received the staunch support of the governing body, led by George Belgrave, himself an Old Combermerian, who had remained devoted to the school. In the end, after deciding to implement all of the clauses of the 1981 Act, in defiance of the amendments urged by the Head teachers' Association, the ministry of education dismissed the governing bodies of the grammar schools and replaced them with new boards of management after March 1983. Combermere's governing body's last official act was to approve the appointment of Harold Wharton as the head of English.[16]

In accordance with the stipulations of the new Education Act, Combermere was attached, for administrative purposes, to Ellerslie Secondary School and the St Leonard's Boys' and Girls' Schools. Marcia Rudder, the secretary/treasurer of the old Combermere school governing body, was appointed secretary/treasurer of these four schools. Under the new scheme, these schools were to have a single secretariat comprising the secretary/treasurer, executive officers, and clerk/typists.[17]

The new board of management consisted of Mrs Edna Scott (chairperson), Percy Chenery, Horace King, Gordon Medford, Sheila Pilgrim, Girwood Springer, Sam Wilkinson, Clyde Williams, and Senator John Williams. They held their inaugural meeting on 22 June 1983 and set up several subcommittees to investigate various aspects of the life of the school.[18]

Almost at once the new board had to consider the case of Pilgrim's alleged illegal admission of a student transferring from the Garrison Secondary School. The headmaster explained the bases of the admission which he and his predecessors had traditionally followed and recommended that, if only for psychological reasons, the student be allowed to remain at Combermere. The board of management voted to let the student and twelve other similar transfers remain, pledged that no comparable infractions would be repeated, and requested the ministry to send the schools registered copies of the vital new guidelines.[19]

It was the continuing rigidity of the ministry of education which gradually persuaded the board of management to support Pilgrim's cause. Even on such a small matter as the granting of a half holiday to celebrate David Jean-Marie's triumph in the Barbados Scholarship examinations there was a squabble. Whereas Major Noott, in 1956, had granted the school a half holiday to mark Keith A.P. Sandiford's winning of an exhibition to the UCWI, Pilgrim was now denied the right to make a similar gesture for a greater achievement a few generations later.[20] In the face of such inflexibility, the board of management voted to defend Pilgrim in his suit against the ministry and to help him secure legal counsel. They demanded to know from the minister of education what provision she was prepared to make to pay for such counsel.[21] They also rejected the ministry's request, without considering adequate provision for additional space and staff, to admit 150 new students in 1984.[22]

When the subcommittees reported very favourably on the school's work, the members of the board of management were all the more determined to cooperate fully with Pilgrim. They were much impressed by the wide range of extracurricular activity in which the staff encouraged the students to participate. They were now therefore prepared to recommend additional toilet facilities for students and staff, repairs to laboratories and pavilions, provision of hard courts for such games as tennis and netball, and urgent repairs to the school's electrical system. Sheila Pilgrim, who chaired one of the subcommittees, expressed her total satisfaction with the organization of the Combermere School Cadet Company and the growth of the impressive Cadet Band. The subcommittee which inspected the buildings and the grounds showed considerable concern for the health and sanitation of the school and insisted that there should be toilet facilities for the boys in a ratio of 1:45 and 1:35 for the girls.[23]

Combermere was performing well in many areas despite the multitude of problems and difficulties being encountered. A large number of these problems stemmed from the changed status brought about by the Education Act (1981). It was perhaps inevitable that the transition period would be a difficult one, for Combermere had operated within a tradition of almost full autonomy. The ministry of education had now become responsible for appointments, dismissals and leaves. But it had seriously extended its functions without correspondingly increasing its staff. Many tasks consequently remained undone and some urgent assignments were addressed too tardily. Too often, important timetabling decisions could not be completed because schools were awaiting final approval from the ministry even after the academic session had commenced. In 1985, for example, some Combermere teachers actually returned from leave and resumed duty before their leave was officially approved.[24]

These were the kinds of problems with which Pilgrim was confronted and which led to a good deal of frustration on his part. The perception that head teachers no longer controlled staffing, curricula, or even discipline led to the feeling that their authority was severely undermined. This in turn eroded their confidence and occasionally created the feeling that their position was almost untenable. The Combermere headship thus became too ambiguous an office for a man so forthright and uncomplicated as Pilgrim. He accepted an offer to head a secondary school in the British Virgin Islands and tendered his resignation in 1986.

Pilgrim, however, might have given up a trifle too soon for in the general elections of May that same year there was a change of government and Erskine Sandiford, who later became prime minister of Barbados after Errol Barrow's death in 1987, now took over the education portfolio. He tried to defuse the feelings of tension and resentment which had developed amongst the general teaching body and suggested a review of the Education Act that had brought about such unease. He replaced the new board of management with the old administrative team, led again by Belgrave, whose relationship with Pilgrim had always been cordial. Both men were driven by a keen desire to make Combermere the finest school in the country. Hence they often saw eye to eye and worked well together. Indeed close cooperation between staff and governing body had been the main feature of Combermere's history for at least ten years prior to 1983.

It is, of course, too much to expect that any government will abandon the notion of centralization in the educational system. Governments, after all, spend gigantic sums on education every year and will want to know that these sums are being effectively and efficiently used. Whereas the total Combermere budget in 1950 was approximately $87,000,[25] it had grown to $181,000 by 1960.[26] Then came the series of salary revisions and increases which conspired with spiralling costs to drive the Combermere annual expenditures beyond $700,000 by 1975.[27] The million dollar mark was eclipsed in 1980-81 and, by the time of Pilgrim's resignation, the draft estimates for 1986-87 projected a Combermere bill of about $2.8 million. In the academic year 1991-92 the actual budget had exceeded $3 million.[28] No government can consistently allocate such huge sums to institutions without somehow trying to supervise the manner in which the institutions are run and the money is being spent. Even so, if schools are to function efficiently and effectively, a

C.W. Pilgrim, Headmaster 1981–86

certain amount of authority and power must reside within the school, with clear lines of accountability and communication with the ministry of education.

Pilgrim created such an impression on the majority of those who watched him in operation that it is hard to imagine that his tenure of the headship lasted only five years. He gave the school a sense of purpose and direction after twenty years of mediocre leadership. For whereas Pilgrim had a clear notion of where he wanted the school to go and what should be done to get it there, neither Gittens nor Moore articulated a clear vision or philosophy for their school. Pilgrim also used a participative leadership style involving his staff in the decision making process. Gittens, on the other hand, tended to be autocratic and Moore was almost totally *laissez-faire*. Pilgrim's popularity with students and staff was such that few wanted him to quit when he did. In fact, a tremendous fuss was made over him throughout the summer of 1986 after he had announced his resignation. There were farewell banquets and gifts in profusion and abundant indeed was the praise heaped upon him from every quarter. The rapport which he had established with colleagues, pupils and members of the board of mangement was transparently obvious. During the Combermere School Old Scholars' Week in October 1986, whenever he had occasion to revisit the school, the boys and girls gave him prolonged and spontaneous ovations. The depth of their feeling could not have been missed even by the most casual observer. When the Old Scholars held a cocktail party in the middle of that week, Charlie's contemporaries showed their appreciation by repeatedly singing the well-known Pilgrim Hymn "He who would valiant be", which has now become almost an adjunct to the traditional school song. Charles W. Pilgrim had, after all, rendered to Combermere School thirty-three years of unbroken and meritorious service. No doubt, in due course, there will be some kind of plaque or memorial unveiled at Waterford as a tribute to him. Indeed similar tributes also need to be paid to such persons as Harry Sealy and the late Frank Collymore for their illustrious contributions to Combermere and the wider community.

The Advent of Keith Roach

Pilgrim's work was continued by Keith Roach, who was first appointed deputy headmaster in 1981. He was promptly named acting headmaster in 1986 and after a brief interval was offered the headship on 1 January 1987. 'Spoonie', as Roach has always been called by his friends, was born on 22 June 1936 and had first entered Combermere School as a pupil in January 1946 during Armstrong's last year as headmaster. The next year he proceeded to Harrison College where he remained until 1955. He finally returned to Combermere as an assistant master under Gittens in September 1966 and rose to the headship of the English department in the early 1970s. He was one of the catalysts who had helped to keep the staff together at a difficult period in the school's history. So too was Dorien Pile, who was now appointed acting deputy head teacher on 1 September 1986 and would later be confirmed in that post on 1 April 1987.

Roach's educational background and training are similar to Pilgrim's and there was little possibility that he would have attempted to undo his predecessor's work. In any case, by 1986, the headmaster's role had become more circumscribed and it was now not as straightforward for a headteacher to impose his or her stamp upon an institution in the same manner in which previous educators had been able to do. Nonetheless, Keith Roach has made quite an impression on the administration of the school. As deputy headmaster under Charlie Pilgrim he was responsible for much of the innovation in curriculum and administration which has permitted Combermere to stand out as a dynamic institution. Now, as head, he has continued in this vein and in this he is ably assisted by Dorien Pile.

Roach introduced both at CXC and Advanced level a range of new subjects which boosted the business studies programme. Combermere had led the way earlier in this field. CXC accounts, office procedures and principles of business would deepen into advanced level accounts and economics. Social studies which was firmly established throughout the lower school could be studied more intensively as sociology at Advanced level.

The interest in, and demand for, these new offerings both from within the student body and from non-Combermerian sixth form applicants underlined the need for administrators to keep their schools in a dynamic equilibrium with the society's and the students' needs. A wider range of choice and combination of subjects was made available from the third to fifth forms. For example, students could now easily combine the study of physics and art or chemistry and music. The talented could satisfactorily study both, in a changed administrative climate.

Some of the senior staff who served Roach's three predecessors have either retired or moved on to other avenues of employment. But the general stability and cohesiveness of the staff have permitted many successful innovations to be carried out. The success in academic areas has continued and intensified. CXC results have shown significant improvements both in quality and quantity. While in the 1970s a student with eight subject passes at one sitting was a rarity, more than 60% of the students entered attained that standard in the early 1990s.

The school has seen the extension of science facilities, built from savings and with little disruption during school time. This has finally met a need articulated regularly across two decades. Roach permits his staff to suggest and implement worthwhile projects with minimum supervision. The school's external environment bears testimony to the work and commitment of teachers like Dorien Pile, Monica Peter-Newlands and Annette Jebodhsingh who have been working to cultivate environmental awareness in the students and ancillary staff long before this was fashionable in the society.

The number and range of extracurricular activities have grown during this period. The school now offers over twenty-five different activities. Most students can find (a teacher and) an activity to spark a long lasting interest. This is in keeping with Roach's vision of the "complete" Combermerian. Success in a wider range of sports is part of this broadening of the base seen during the current administration. Combermere continues to contribute cricketers and hockey players to the national teams. But badminton and volleyball have recently caught the students' imagination and the nation's interest.

Keith Roach is a firm disciplinarian. Both students and staff are constantly reminded of their obligations to develop self-discipline. His strong sense of what it is to be a Combermerian is conveyed to the school body by example and exhortation. Often the latter is enough to maintain an ordered but non-threatening environment in which growth can take place. While it may be too early to assess Roach's work at Combermere, growth has certainly been its hallmark. Combermere has maintained its tradition as a fine school. Parents' choice underlines this, pupils' performance bears this out, and dedicated and loyal alumni ensure its survival.

Combermere has had a history of maintaining the loyalty of its workers through thick and thin. Thus, for instance, it has had only six head porters, all of whom came through the ranks, since 1913. Clement held the position for twenty years before his death in 1933; Toppin then carried the torch for another quarter of a century, before passing it on to Headley; and Bowen, first hired by Noott as one of Toppin's assistants in 1947, retired in November 1988 at the age of sixty. He was succeeded by Small [29] who has in turn been succeeded by Frank Reveira. All of these individuals became ardently

The Principal, K.A. Roach (extreme right), Deputy Principal, Mrs. D. Pile (left) with Ian Sinckler, Karl Broodhagen and a student preparing to celebrate the school's 300th anniversary

Combermerian in their outlook and took pride in the achievements of *their* students.

While one can easily understand Bowen's attachment to Combermere, it is much more difficult to explain the devotion of such individuals as Pilgrim and Roach. Bowen, after all, spent the vast bulk of his adult life working for a single institution. It is supremely ironic that both Pilgrim and Roach have become dedicated Combermerians despite the fact that they had spent many years as pupils at Harrison College. Roach had spent only five terms altogether as a student at Combermere, as compared with the eight years he studied at Harrison College. But he has always remained proud of his Combermere roots and was very happy to join its staff in 1966. He has always considered himself a Combermerian first and foremost. Like Pilgrim, he is totally devoted to the school and is anxious to see it prosper.[30]

That Combermere is prospering there can be no doubt whatsoever. The school's reputation is as high now as it ever was. Entrance into its walls is eagerly sought after and its public image is much enhanced by the well-known activities of its alumni. It is no longer (as it was in Armstrong's time) the largest school in Barbados, but that does not matter. Its reputation is based on the quality of its teaching and the richness of its heritage. And it has held its own in an increasingly complicated arena. Whereas there were only thirteen or fourteen government secondary schools in Barbados as late as 1961, there are now twenty-two, catering to the needs of about 22,000 students. The competition, that is to say, has grown in a series of remarkable strides from the time that the government became more committed to the principle of free secondary training for all of those children capable of competing successfully in Common Entrance Examinations.

The liberal education policy placed Barbados far ahead of almost every other community in its willingness to provide elementary and secondary education for its youth. When, in the mid-1980s, Barbados was devoting almost 25% of its annual expenditures to education, this was more than any other nation was then prepared to do. By stark contrast, the mighty United States was at that time devoting less than 4% of its revenues to this important field. This meant that Barbados was spending far more per capita on education than any of its contemporaries. Not surprisingly, then, Barbados was classed among the most literate of all societies. This is in keeping with a long-standing Barbadian tradition.

This is the context in which Pilgrim and Roach have been operating. Their school, like dozens of other academic institutions, was consuming increasingly large chunks of public money and the government felt it had no choice but to centralize the system. The price paid for additional funding was increasing bureaucratic interference and control. But Roach's progressive attitude towards programmes and curricula suggests that there is still room for individual initiative on the part of modern principals.

Like all other secondary schools, Combermere has to cope with bureaucratic constraints as well as shifting disciplines and rapidly changing societal needs. Even an ancient secondary school, in these days of keen competition and constant change, can find itself left far behind if it is feebly administered from within. Subjects which suffered from benign neglect in a former age must now be studied with the same earnestness that was once reserved for the classics and the humanities. Microcomputers, for instance, were unknown in the age of Noott. It is unlikely that any academic institution can now ignore computer science and engineering. The importance of psychology and sociology was not generally acknowledged until very recently. Racism and sexism, once basic features of the Barbadian ethos, are now generally frowned upon. In short, Barbados in the mid-1990s is radically different from the Barbados of 1960. These changes present major challenges to individuals as well as institutions. Pilgrim, Roach and Combermere have met their challenges head-on.

Chapter Seven

Epilogue

Attitudes such as those displayed by Pilgrim and Roach tell us a great deal about Combermere, particularly since the age of Noott. The school has captured the imagination of the alumni and held it in a truly miraculous way. As Frank Gibbons pointed out, when he was a young man that was not the case. He once had occasion to remark that most Barbadians of his generation were more eager to disavow their Combermere connections and to stress their commitment to one of the first-grade schools.[1] Nowadays, the opposite is true. The attachment to the school is clearly reflected in the fact that its alumni still have the most vibrant association of its kind in Barbados. Indeed, there is also an old and prosperous branch in the United States. The pride in their alma mater is more pronounced among Combermerians than perhaps among past students of any school in Barbados including the old first-grade schools. It is interesting to note that in recent years Combermere affiliations, hitherto kept beneath a bushel, have eagerly been brought out in the light of day. Even the late Errol Barrow, for many years prime minister of Barbados, was wont to boast in his later years that he had spent a term or two at Combermere School with the late Chalmer St Hill, with whom he also shared the same birth date.[2]

For many years Combermere has made a significant contribution to the history and development of Barbados. This is so precisely because the school has invariably tried to keep pace with the social and economic changes in its constantly evolving environment. Thus, when recently manumitted Blacks and Coloureds sought education in the nineteenth century, it gradually opened its doors to them in a way that contemporary institutions were not yet prepared to do. When it was designated a second-grade secondary school in the late 1870s, it steadily rearranged its programmes and curricula to meet the needs of an emerging bourgeoisie, while the first-grade schools continued to cater to the needs of a more conservative élite. Harrison College and the Lodge School seemed content to prepare its brightest pupils for careers in medicine, religion, law and education. The avowed philosophy of Combermere's administrative leaders, from the very beginning, was to prepare *all* of its students, in a pragmatic fashion, to make useful contributions of every sort to the life and culture of the wider community.

Predictably, therefore, Old Combermerians have starred in every conceivable arena, both in Barbados and beyond. An impressive list of earlier generations of Old Combermerians appears in the unpublished papers of the late Frank Gibbons. In the political field, for example, there is Wynter A. Crawford, one of the leading civil rights activists of the interwar years who founded, edited and published the *Barbados Observer* for the purpose of drawing attention to the injustices and inequalities within the sociopolitical system. He served in the House of Assembly continuously from the early 1940s into the 1960s until his resignation from the ruling DLP over his principled position with respect to the Little Eight.[3] His contribution to labour legislation and his efforts to rally the sugar workers for positive action are well-known. Equally well-known are the contributions of Chrissie Brathwaite, George Ferguson, Elsworth Holder, Fred Miller and Hilton Vaughan. In more recent times, the composition of the DLP cabinets (1986–94) is eloquent testimony of the school's impact in this regard. Such former ministers as Harold Blackman, Dr Carl Clarke, Warwick Franklyn, Wesley Hall, Harcourt Lewis, Keith Simmons, Brandford Taitt, David Thompson and Cyril Walker are all full-fledged Combermerians. Lawson Weekes, Speaker of the House in the last government (1991-94), was amongst the very first intake at first form level of Major Noott in January 1947, an honour he shares with another former parliamentarian, Amory Phillips. The current Speaker, Ishmael Roett, is also a Combermerian.

Frank Collymore who served the School for many years

Key positions in the security services, the Barbados Defence Force (BDF) and its forerunner the Barbados Regiment, and the Royal Barbados Police Force (RBPF) have for a long time been filled by Old Combermerians. Colonel Walcott and Colonel Leonard Banfield, for example, have been successively commanding Officers of the Barbados Regiment. The former was the first black Barbadian to hold the post, the latter went on to become the first chief of staff of the BDF on its establishment. Orville Durant, a well-qualified attorney-at-law and Commissioner of the RBPF since 1982, and Lt Colonel Deighton Maynard, Deputy Chief of Staff of the BDF are both Combermerians of the Noott era. In both of these organizations, there are many Old Scholars filling senior ranks.

In the field of religion, law and particularly in education and the civil service, Combermerians have given and continue to give great service. The few examples which follow are cited by way of illustration. The outspoken and ofttimes controversial Dean Harold Crichlow of the St Michael Cathedral; Mr Justice Errol Chase, retired Justice Lindsay Worrell and Solicitor-General Woodbine Davis; and a number of successful attorneys, present and former permanent secretaries, and other high ranking civil servants-Orville Belle (Commissioner of Inland Revenue), Walter Burke, Sam Corbin, Edward Layne, Henderson Richards, Denis Smith (permanent secretaries), Chalmer St Hill (public librarian), Kenneth Pile and Harold White (Commissioners of Land Tax); Registrar at the Cave Hill Campus of the University of the West Indies, Andrew Lewis; and a number of academic staff such as Dr Desmond Clarke, Dr Andrew Downes, Dr Stephen Harewood, Dr Michael Howard, Wendell Maclean, Professor Earle Newton, Dr Carl Wade and many teachers across the nation's schools.

Combermere's contribution to Barbadian culture especially since the appointment of Broodhagen and Millington in the 1940s has simply been incalculable. Almost every artist or musician produced in Barbados over the past forty years or so has been trained by these two outstanding men or by teachers taught by them. Their influence on West Indian art and music can never be exaggerated. Equally significant is Frank Collymore's contribution to and influence on West Indian literature. It was he who encouraged and inspired authors across the Caribbean such as Austin Clarke, George Lamming (himself an Old Combermerian), Harold Marshall, Edgar Mittelholtzer, Eric Roach, Karl Sealy, Derek Walcott and John Wickham, by publishing their early work in the various issues of *Bim*, the pioneer among West Indian literary journals.[4] Many of his protégés have achieved international prominence in the field of literature.

Few schools anywhere could have had the same impact as Combermere has had on the history of cricket. Over the years it has produced a long line of cricket stars who have made their contribution at the local, regional or international levels. Perhaps such cricketers as Denis and Eric Atkinson, Rawle Brancker, 'Snuffie' Browne, George Carew, Herman Griffith, Wes Hall, E.L.G. Hoad Sr., Peter Lashley, 'Mannie' Martindale, Derek Sealy and 'Foffie' Williams are all sufficiently well-known to the cricket enthusiast and historian in Barbados and beyond as to require no introduction. David Archer, a highly respected umpire in international cricket, was an Old Combermerian. The school can also boast of having produced in John Holder not only an English County cricketer but more particularly the first black umpire on England's Test match panel. However, the school's most significant contribution to cricket anywhere must be beyond a shadow of a doubt the renowned Sir Frank Worrell, perhaps the chief architect of modern West Indian cricket dominance on the international stage.[5]

Yet, it is still arguable that Combermere's greatest legacy to Barbadian society has been its contribution to the field of business and commerce. Ever since the days of Burton and Speed, Combermere has maintained a reputation for producing the clerical and commercial minds who have dominated the businesses and industries of Bridgetown. The list of Combermerians who left their mark on Barbadian trade and commerce is truly remarkable. Among many others, it includes the late St Clair Hunte, Vernon Knight, Freddie Miller and Bruce Weatherhead. More currently, Rawle Brancker (Brancker & Co. Ltd), Amory Phillips (Barbados Lumber Co.) and Basil Sandiford (Berger Paints Ltd) are making enormous contributions to the business life of the Barbadian community. Between 1850 and 1930 Combermere did more than any other single institution to staff the factories, foundries, plantations and department stores of the country. Today it continues to supply personnel who make a positive contribution to the society at all levels and in all walks of life.

A school that has achieved so much and contributed so significantly to the development of any nation, deserves a place in the recorded history of that nation. Few institutions of its kind can ever have been so utterly dominant in so many diverse fields. Combermere has virtually set the tone for all features of Barbadian life during the period of independence. That it has done so is largely due to its traditional image. It has historically been perceived as the one major institution catering to the needs and interests of the lower-middle and poorer strata of Barbadian society. As such, it always somehow seemed to convey the impression that it was leading the rebellion against the tyranny of élitism and privilege. Thus, even during the lean decades of the interwar period, Combermerians under Burton, Cox and Armstrong expressed a certain yearning for emancipation by aggressively challenging the élite on the playground and in the classroom. Even without adequate playing fields or equipment, they could therefore win several championships at the interschool sports and the vast majority of the first-grade exhibitions. Their athletic triumphs in the 1930s and 1940s were all the more impressive since the students of the first-grade schools remained two years longer than Combermerians were then allowed to do. Until the introduction of the sixth form by Noott, Combermerians had to leave school by the time they were eighteen years old. This had placed their division one athletes, cricketers, and other teams at a substantial disadvantage.

After independence in 1966, Combermere came to serve as a curious kind of symbol. It represented the new and vibrant bourgeoisie and stood triumphantly and unmistakably for modern Black pride. Harrison College and the Lodge School initially representing the white élite, while only admitting a small number of Blacks (especially after 1920) inevitably underwent a change of identity and meaning as they were only then beginning to really straddle the boundaries of class and colour. This uncertain position could be considered to have affected their legitimacy as a symbol for any clearly identifiable group or cause.

That Combermere has never suffered from any such metamorphosis may partly have been due both to its origin and the fact that the vast majority of its headmasters have been born in Barbados. Prior to 1961, all of Combermere's headmasters had been white, but most of them had the inestimable advantage of being natives, unlike their counterparts at Harrison College. They could thus identify more readily with their students. The outstanding exception to this general rule, curiously enough, was Major Noott; but as he himself confessed, it was his stint in India and Burma during the Second World War that destroyed forever any notions of White supremacy. He came therefore to Barbados with none of that irritating snobbery and blatant racism which had unfortunately characterized the work of Harrison College headmasters prior to 1965 (when Albert Williams became the first non-white Barbadian to be appointed headmaster of that school).[6]

A certain *esprit de corps* is normally developed more rapidly, for obvious reasons, in residential schools. But at the Lodge, which for many years served more or less as a babysitting agency for the wealthiest families across the Caribbean, that *esprit*, so powerful up to the 1930s when the vast bulk of students were white, was gradually undermined by considerations of class and colour. Old Lodge boys who attended that institution in the 1940s still have bitter memories of the blatant racial discrimination they were forced to endure. Excellent cricketers like Sam Headley and Torrey Pilgrim, for instance, were occasionally omitted, without excuse or explanation, from the Lodge School team selected to tour Trinidad for the annual contests against Queen's Royal College (QRC). As late as 1946, there was a great furore, too, when T.L. Evans, the headmaster, promoted Sam Headley to the office of school captain and head prefect. No such outrage had followed the appointment of Harold Brewster to a similar position at Combermere in the previous decade. It is scarcely to be wondered at, then, that Old Combermerians usually have more pleasant memories of their school-days.

Non-Combermerians have never ceased to marvel at the fervent, infectious spirit that infuses not only Combermerians but also virtually everyone that comes into contact with the school by virtue of having worked there. Mrs Grace Pilgrim, wife of Charles Pilgrim, a former headmaster, is in an excellent position to observe it. She was a Queen's College product of the 1950s. While she is devoted to her school, she is always amazed by the depth of feeling unabashedly expressed at CSOSA functions. Perhaps Foundation School might have been expected to develop a similar psychology as it long catered to a similar clientele. It has been teaching lower middle-class children since 1906. But even the Foundation experience has not been the same, even though there have recently emerged two powerful Foundation School Old Scholars' Associations in Toronto, Canada, and London, England. More curious still are the reactions of Old Harrisonians, like Greg Rowe and Archie Yarde, who developed a closer affinity with Combermere, after teaching there for a few years, than they had felt for their own alma mater. Nigel Bradshaw, and Old Lodge boy, and Alfred St John, a Coleridge-Parry product, similarly placed, experienced the identical phenomenon.[7]

These attitudes are best explained by a most perceptive observation once made by another Old Harrisonian, Harold Marshall, for many years (1972-94) the communications officer for the Winnipeg School Division No.1 in the province of Manitoba, Canada. He regretted that his own alma mater had too long been led by British expatriates who were too arrogant in their treatment of black students. They also tended to appoint white English teachers with whom the students seldom empathized. Thus Marshall himself feels that he owes a greater debt to Frank Collymore, the Old Combermerian who encouraged him to write short stories, than to any of his teachers at Harrison College during the 1940s.[8]

Combermere's remarkable *esprit* has been generated over the years by the tendency of Old Combermerians to return to their school as teachers. Its staff has always included a substantial number of its alumni. Thus Combermere has had long and faithful service from such former pupils as Ben Browne, Frank Collymore, C.F.A. Corbin, Dennis Goddard, Gladstone Holder, Deighton Maynard, Ralph Perkins, Colvin Pile, Harry Sealy, Chalmer St Hill and V.B. Williams. Among the current staff are such long serving past students as Eversley, Charles Reid, Patrick Skeete, and Harcourt Wason. Far from being problematic, this inbreeding has been positively healthy. It has helped to strengthen and perpetuate ties of loyalty which motivate individuals to make such sacrifices as become necessary from time to time, that outsiders might not easily make.

Combermere has also profited from the Old Boys' habit of serving on its governing body or board of management. The dedication of such men as Charles G. Alleyne, George Belgrave, Errol Chase, Desmond Clarke, Frank Collymore, Wesley Hall, Fred Miller, Erskine Simmons and Hilton Vaughan has done much over the years to maintain and enhance the lofty traditions and good name of the school.

This flame has burnt brightly not only in Barbados but in many parts of the world. Even now, an Old Combermerian, the Rt Rev. Wilfred Denis Wood, is serving as the bishop of Croydon in Surrey. He is the first black Anglican priest to be promoted to such high office in Britain. Bishop Wood was trained at Combermere in the age of Noott. He was actually the school's cricket captain during 1953-54. Other Old Combermerians are making their mark as scholars in North America. Professor Keith A.P. Sandiford, for instance, has taught history at three Canadian universities during the past thirty years. Dr E.H. Morris Blenman and Dr Winston Nicholls are also rendering yeoman service in Canadian universities, while Dr Keith Albert Sandiford, Associate Professor of English at Louisiana State University, has already begun to make a name for himself by publishing his first literary text, *Measuring the Moment*. There are other Old Combermerians in Canada making a significant contribution to the civil services there. Frank A. Maynard has risen to the post of deputy minister, Department of Health in the province of Manitoba. In Winnipeg, too, William Pitt and Stirling Walkes have become important senior administrators in the provincial civil service. Gregg Edwards, who had much to do with the success of the *Centre Linguistique* in Ottawa, Ontario, is now senior special projects manager with Public Works Canada in that city. For many years, until his recent retirement, Ken Holder was an important bureaucrat in Toronto.

Combermerians can be found making a useful contribution in all worthwhile areas of human endeavour from the humble to the very elevated. They are in Barbados, the wider Caribbean and beyond. It has been said that one sure way to judge a successful, effective school is by looking at the quality of its products and their contribution to human development over a long period of time. There is no doubt that Combermere can successfully withstand the most careful scrutiny and proudly stand as a highly successful and effective school. Combermerians stand poised to celebrate its tercentenary with justifiable pride and enthusiasm and to "keep the flame burning brightly ever".

Notes

CHAPTER ONE

1. Combermere School: its growth and development", *Barbados Evening Advocate*, 18 February 1952. This lengthy article, possibly written by F.A. Hoyos, is a useful source on Combermere's early history. See also the *Combermerian, 1930-31*: 13-14. This detailed account of the school's origins (pp. 13-26) was written by H.G. Hutchinson, a careful researcher, who is still the best guide on this question. In this article he corrected a number of slips which had appeared in G.B.R. Burton's history of the school in the first two issues of the *Combermere School Magazine*, 1913-14.
2. See *Recopied Wills* (Department of Archives, Barbados), RB 3, vol. 18: 345-49. Cited also in the *Journal of the Barbados Museum and Historical Society* XXI (August 1954): 13-16.
3. *Combermerian 1930-31*: 13-16.
4. Ibid., 18.
5. See *Recopied Deeds* (Department of Archives, Barbados), RB 3, vol. 49, no. 1730. There is an interesting notation there, beginning on folio D and continued on folio G, on the relationship between this deed and the original Combermere site. It is dated 1963.
6. *Combermerian 1930-31*: 17.
7. Hutchinson was apparently able to consult the vestry records for the eighteenth century but the majority of these are now unfortunately closed to the public.
8. *Combermerian 1930-31*: 18-21. See also the *Barbados Evening Advocate*, 18 February 1952.
9. *Combermere School Magazine*, June 1913: 3; *Combermerian* 1930-31: 21.
10. J. Gilmore, "Episcopacy, emancipation, and evangelization", (Seminar paper no.6, 1983-84, University of the West Indies, Cave Hill, 1984), 21-27.
11. *Barbados Advocate*, 22 February 1927: 12; J.E. Reece and C.G. Clark-Hunt, eds. *Barbados Diocesan History* (London, 1927), 68. See also F.A. Hoyos, *Barbados: A History from the Amerindians to Independence* (London, 1988), 140-4.

12. *Combermere School Magazine*, June 1913: 3. See also *Laws of Barbados*, 18 January 1822: 119-22.
13. A.E. Dyson & J. Lovelock, eds., *Education and Democracy* (London, 1975), 19-21; R.J. Evans, ed., *Social Policy 1830-1914: Industrialization, Collectivism and the Origins of the Welfare State* (London, 1978), 242; Sir E.L. Woodward, *The Age of Reform: 1815-70* (Oxford, 1962), 478.
14. *Combermere School Magazine*, June 1913: 3.
15. Ibid.
16. *Barbadoes* [sic] *Blue Book* 1833, 126-7.
17. Celia Karch, "London Bourne of Barbados"(Paper presented at the Fifteenth Conference of Caribbean Historians, University of the West Indies, Mona, April 1983), 20; S. Leslie, "Education for girls in Barbados in 1850"(Seminar paper no.8, 1983-84, University of the West Indies, Cave Hill, 1984), 29.
18. *Barbados Blue Book 1846*, 138.
19. *Barbados Blue Book 1848*, 137.
20. *Barbados Blue Book 1850*, 152-3; *Combermere School Magazine*, Oct. 1913: 2.
21. *Combermere School Magazine, First Term 1914-15: 2; Combermerian 1930-31: 21.*
22. *Barbados Blue Book*, 1851, 136; *Barbados Blue Book*, 1846, 138.
23. *Barbados Blue Book*, 1851, 137.
24. *Combermerian 1930-31:* 21.
25. Ibid., *Combermere School Magazine*, First Term 1914-15: 2.
26. *Combermere School Magazine*, Second Term 1914-15: 2.
27. Barbados, *Commission on Education Report 1875*, 35.
28. Ibid., 7.
29. Ibid., 20-6; N. Greenhalgh, "Education in Barbados", in Reece & Clark-Hunt, eds., 69-70; T.W. Heyck, *The Peoples of the British Isles: From 1870 to the Present* (California, 1992), 90-1.
30. *Commission Report 1875*, 8.
31. *Barbados Blue Book 1873*, U2.
32. *Combermerian 1930-31:* 21.
33. *Greenhalgh*, 70.
34. *Barbados Blue Book 1899*, U24-6.
35. *Colony of Barbados 1901*, U24, U26.
36. *Barbados Agricultural Reporter*, 21 July 1896; *Barbados Advocate*, 23 April 1923; *Combermere School Magazine*, Third Term 1915-16: 2.
37. Barbados, *Education Commission Report 1894*, 25.
38. Bruce Hamilton, *Cricket in Barbados* (Bridgetown, 1947), 12; Philip Thorn, *Barbados Cricketers, 1865-1990* (Nottingham, 1991), 18, 29. See also Keith A.P. Sandiford & Brian Stoddart, "The elite schools and cricket in Barbados: a study

in colonial continuity", *The International Journal of the History of Sport* (December 1987): 337.
39. *Commission Report 1894*, 25.
40. Ibid. *Education Commission Report 1875*, 21; *Barbados Blue Book 1874*, U1; *Barbados Blue Book 1883*, U19-20.
41. *Barbados Blue Book 1889*, U19-20.
42. *Barbados Blue Book 1894*, N83-4.
43. Ibid., N84. *Barbados Blue Book 1895*, N84.
44. *Barbados Blue Book 1895*, N84. See also *Education Commission Report 1875*, 41; and *Education Commission Report 1894*, 25.
45. Bentley Gibbs, "Government and the problem of social reconstruction, 1838-1849" (Seminar paper no.3, 1976-77, University of the West Indies, Cave Hill 1976): 20-22; Anthony DeV. Phillips, "The racial factor in politics in Barbados 1880-1914" (Seminar paper, University of the West Indies, Cave Hill, n.d.): 13-14.
46. *Barbados Blue Book 1892*, U20.
47. Keith A.P. Sandiford, "Education and the Barbadian society", *Banja: A Magazine of Barbadian Life and Culture* (April 1989): 45. See also the *Blue Books* for the period 1880-1900.
48. *Barbados Blue Book 1895*, C4-6.
49. *Education Commission Report 1894*, 34.
50. *Barbados Blue Book 1896*, U24.
51. Ibid., U23-4.
52. *Combermerian 1928-29*, 21.
53. See, for example, Woodward, *Age of Reform*, passim.
54. The question of the Barbadians' refusal to follow the moderate counsels of the imperial government throughout the nineteenth century has been well documented by such scholars as Gibbs, in "Government and the problem of social reconstruction"; Phillips, in "The racial factor in politics in Barbados"; and Vaughan, in "The shaping of the new order".
55. F.A. Hoyos, *From the Amerindians to Independence*, 143.
56. Celia Karch, "London Bourne of Barbados", passim.; Glen O. Phillips, "The beginnings of Samuel J. Prescod, 1806-43: Afro-Barbadian civil rights crusader and activist", *The Americas: A Quarterly Review of Inter-American Cultural History* 38, no.3 (January 1982): passim.
57. *Laws of Barbados*, 24 October 1850, 458-9.
58. Ibid., 21 December 1858, 123.
59. Ibid., 9 December 1878, 165-209; Rev. J.E. Reece, et al., "The system of education in Barbados" [1902] in Board of Education, *Special Reports on Educational Subjects* XII (London, 1968): 44-7.

60. Even as late as Resolution 83/1945 — amendment to 12/1890, the Scheme of Government for Combermere School left its headmaster with considerable authority.
61. *Combermerian 1928-29*, 48.
62. Philip Thorn, 14.

CHAPTER TWO

1. *Combermere School Magazine*, Third Term 1915-16: 2; *Barbados Advocate*, 24 April 1897.
2. *Barbados Advocate*, 22 August 1896: 7.
3. Ibid., 3 September 1896: 6; *Harrisonian*, July 1922: 44-5.
4. *Combermere School Magazine*, First Term 1925-26: 9-10.
5. Ibid., Second Term 1920-21: 7.
6. Ibid., Third Term 1922-23: 10. See also Ibid., 1920-26.
7. *Barbados Advocate*, 3 December 1897: 6.
8. Ibid., 8 December 1897: 6.
9. Ibid., 7 December 1897: 6; and 11 December 1897: 9.
10. Ibid., 7 April 1900: 5.
11. Ibid., 24 April 1900: 5.
12. Ibid., 12 April 1901: 6.
13. Ibid., 25 May 1901: 5.
14. *Combermere School Magazine*, Third Term 1918-19: 2.
15. See, e.g., *Barbados Advocate*, 8 August 1901: 5-6.
16. *Legislative Debates*, Barbados, House of Assembly, 16 December 1902, 225-8.
17. *Barbados Advocate*, 18 December 1902: 5.
18. Ibid., 4 May 1903: 8-10.
19. Ibid., 5 May 1903: 5; and 8 August 1903: 6. See also the *Barbados Blue Book 1903-04*: U24.
20. *Combermere School Magazine*, Third Term 1917-18: 15.
21. *Barbados Advocate*, 8 August 1903: 6-7.
22. Ibid., 27 April 1908: 5; *Barbados Blue Book 1903-04*: U24-28.
23. *Lodge School Record*, 1926: 5.
24. *Barbados Advocate*, 18 December 1909: 8.
25. *Barbados Blue Book 1903-04*: D1-3; Sandiford, "Education and the Barbadian society", 45.
26. Phillips, "The racial factor in politics in Barbados", 14.
27. Barbados. *Education Commission Report 1907-09* (Bridgetown, 1909), 2-3.
28. *Barbados Agricultural Reporter*, 26 October 1905: 2.

29. *Commission Report 1907-09*, 17-19.
30. Ibid., 19.
31. Ibid.
32. *Colony of Barbados 1910-11*, N85. *Colony of Barbados 1911-12*, N85.
33. *Barbados Advocate*, 5 May 1903: 5.
34. "Extracts from minutes of the Combermere School Governing Body meetings, 1902-25", Frank Leo Gibbons Papers. See also the *Barbados Blue Books* for the period 1895-1915.
35. See, e.g., Frank Collymore, "My schooldays", in *Combermerian*, undated (1973?): 14.
36. *Advocate Year Book and Who's Who 1951* (Bridgetown, 1951): 197-233.
37. J.G. Wilson to M.T.G. Mahon, 25 April 1932, Combermere School Records; and Combermere School Paysheets 1932, ibid.
38. *Combermere School Magazine*, 1925-26: 1.
39. Ibid., Second Term 1924-25: 1; *Combermerian* 1944-45: 10; Combermere School Paysheets 1944-45.
40. Frank Collymore File, Combermere School Records.
41. L.L. Webster File, ibid; Headmaster's Speech Day Address, 19 July 1950, ibid.
42. M.T.G. Mahon to A.E. Armstrong, 22 July 1936, ibid.
43. *Combermerian* 1928-29: 2; Combermere School Paysheets 1929.
44. *Combermere School Magazine*, December 1964: 42-4; V.B. Williams File, Combermere School Records.
45. Combermere School Paysheets 1955-56; C.F.A. Corbin File, Combermere School Records.
46. *Combermere School Magazine*, Second Term 1914-15: 6.
47. E.g., *Barbados Advocate*, 25 May 1901: 5; and 18 December 1902: 5.
48. *Barbados Agricultural Reporter*, 9 January 1910.
49. On the basis of performance in this examination, scholarships were awarded on a competitive basis to the first-grade schools. It is thanks to this and similar scholarships, also to the second-grade schools e.g. primary to first- or second-grade, that many poor, but bright, students received a secondary education. In this exam, the following subjects were tested: Latin, French, maths and English.
50. Personal interview with F.L. Gibbons, 27 September 1986. See also Barbados, *Education Department Annual Report* (1910-30).
51. *Combermere School Magazine*, October 1913: 7.
52. Ibid., First Term 1914-15: 5.
53. Ibid., Second Term 1916-17: 21.
54. Ibid., Second Term 1917-18: 4.

55. Ibid., Second Term 1918-19: 2.
56. Ibid., Third Term: 13.
57. Ibid., Third Term 1919-20: 5.
58. Ibid., Third Term 1920-21: 7.
59. Ibid., Second Term 1921-22: 3.
60. Ibid., Third Term 1922-23: 10; Second Term 1924-25: 2; *Combermerian 1926-27*: 1.
61. *Combermere School Magazine*, First Term 1922-23: 2.
62. *Combermerian 1926-27*: 1.
63. Frank Gibbons interview, 27 September 1986.
64. *Combermere School Magazine*, June 1913: 6.
65. Ibid: 6-7.
66. Ibid., Second Term 1916-17: 4.
67. Ibid., Third Term 1921-22: 8.
68. Ibid., October 1913: 8.
69. Ibid., June 1913: 7; and Ibid., Third Term 1913-14: 3.
70. Ibid., Third Term 1922-23: 13.
71. Ibid., June 1913: 15.
72. Ibid.
73. Ibid., Second Term 1914-15: 17.
74. Ibid., Third Term 1923-24: 21.
75. Ibid., First Term 1924-25: 14-16.
76. *Barbados Advocate*, 3 September 1896: 6.
77. *Combermere School Magazine*, Third Term 1919-20: 6.
78. Ibid., Third Term 1918-19: 15.
79. Ibid., Second Term 1923-24: 1; *Barbados Advocate*, 9 April 1898: 5.
80. *Combermere School Magazine*, June 1913: 14; and Ibid., Third Term 1913- 14: 13. See also Combermere School Paysheets 1954-56.
81. *Combermere School Magazine*, First Term 1921-22: 2; *Combermerian* 1930- 31: 43; Hamilton, 75; Thorn, passim. See also K.A.P. Sandiford, "The role of Combermere School in the development of cricket in Barbados", *Cricket Lore* (forthcoming).
82. Keith A.P. Sandiford, "Cricket and the Barbadian society", *Canadian Journal of History* 21 (December 1986): 353-70.
83. *Combermere School Magazine*, Third Term 1921-22: 1.
84. Ibid., Second Term 1924-25: 1.
85. Ibid., Third Term 1918-19: 3.
86. Ibid, First Term 1915-16: 17-18; and Second Term 1921-22: 9.
87. Ibid., Third Term 1923-24: 17.

88. Ibid., Third Term 1924-25: 5-6.
89. Ibid., Second Term 1913-14: 5.
90. Ibid., First Term 1916-17: 2-4.
91. This list has been assembled from the files of the *Combermere School Magazine*, 1913-26, *The Advocate Year Book and Who's Who* (Bridgetown, 1951) and the *Barbados Year Book 1964* (Bridgetown, 1964). See also the Frank Gibbons Private Papers, II, n.p. for the impressive list of Old Combermerians who studied under Burton. Gibbons, who died in 1990 at the age of 82, was a retired land surveyor who taught at Combermere School from 1928 to 1947. He was planning to write a history of the school himself but gave up the attempt and very kindly allowed us full access to his private papers in 1986.
92. Frank Collymore, "My schooldays", undated *Combermerian* (1973?): 17; Rev. A.F. Mandeville to Major C.E. Noott, 14 July 1950, Combermere School Records.
93. Frank L. Gibbons interview, 27 September 1986.
94. *Combermerian 1925-26*: 3-4.
95. Ibid., 1949-50: 137-8.
96. Ibid., 1936-37: 1-2; Keith A.P. Sandiford, "Combermere School, 1926-46: twenty years of rapid growth", *Banja: A Magazine of Barbadian Life & Culture 3* (August 1988): 44-53.
97. Hilary Beckles, *A History of Barbados: From Amerindian Settlement to Nation State* (Cambridge, 1990), 143-7.

CHAPTER THREE

1. *Barbados Agricultural Reporter*, 18 September 1897.
2. *Combermerian 1934-35*: 10-11: *Harrisonian*, April 1926: 12-15; and July 1934: 5-6; *Barbados Advocate*, 24 July 1934. See also Sandiford and Stoddart, 338-9.
3. Headmaster's Annual Reports, 1927-34, Combermere School Records.
4. *Combermere School Magazine*, Second Term 1924-25: 1.
5. Frank Gibbons interview, 27 September 1986.
6. Ibid.
7. *Combermerian 1925-26*: 42-3.
8. Gibbons Papers, I, 9.
9. *Combermerian 1927-28*: 3; and 1928-29: 6.
10. *Combermerian 1929-30*: 8; and 1930-31: 3.
11. Headmaster's Reports, 1927-30, Combermere School Records. See also Gibbons Papers, II, n.p.
12. *Combermere School Magazine*, Third Term 1918-19: 14.
13. Ibid., 1920-26.

14. *Combermerian 1925-30.*
15. *Barbados Blue Book 1925-26*, 207.
16. George Leslie Armstrong, an Old Harrisonian, left a sum of money to provide scholarships for poor children who were also physically and intellectually promising to enable them to obtain a secondary education at Harrison College. The first Scholarship was awarded in 1927. With the advent of free secondary education, the Scholarship lost some of its significance. "The Bequest of George Leslie Armstrong", *The Harrisonian 1933-1993*, the 250th Anniversary Issue.
17. H.B.G. Austin to G.B.Y. Cox, 29 July 1927; and G.B.Y. Cox to H.B.G. Austin, 30 July 1927, Combermere School Records.
18. See the *Barbados Blue Books* for the period 1920-27.
19. Headmaster's Reports, 1927-34, Combermere School Records.
20. L.C.G. Taggart to M.T.G. Mahon, 11 June 1928 and 22 April 1929, ibid.
21. *Barbados Estimates 1931-32*, 1-2.
22. Frank Gibbons interview, 27 September 1986. See also Gibbons Papers, II, n.p.
23. Combermere School Paysheets, 1932, Combermere School Records.
24. M.T.G. Mahon to G.B.Y. Cox, 14 April 1932, ibid.
25. Combermere school staff to the governing body, 30 October 1931, ibid.
26. Gibbons interview, 27 September 1986.
27. Combermere school staff to the governing body, 30 October 1931, Combermere School Records.
28. M.T.G. Mahon to G.B.Y. Cox, 10 May 1932, ibid.
29. Headmaster's Report, 1928-29, ibid.
30. A.E. Armstrong File, ibid. *Advocate Year Book and Who's Who 1951* (Bridgetown, 1951), 198; *Barbados Annual Review 1955*, 71; *Harrisonian*, December 1928: 35.
31. General consensus among the surviving members of Armstrong's staff, interviewed by the authors during the period 1985-88. Armstrong's students also expressed uniformly negative opinions about him.
32. Gibbons interview, 27 September 1986.
33. *Combermerian 1936-37*: 1-2.
34. Ibid., 1942-43: 5; Combermere School Roll, September 1940-July 1941, Combermere School Records.
35. *Lodge School Record*, December 1943: 10.
36. *Harrisonian*, December 1934: 2; and December 1942: 2.
37. E.g., *Combermerian 1936-37*: 10.
38. Governing body to the Education Board, 10 October 1936, Combermere School Records.
39. M.T.G. Mahon to J.T.C. Ramsay, 1 July 1937, ibid.; Major Peck to the Education Board, 8 September 1937, ibid.

40. M.T.G. Mahon to the Director of Public Works, 17 August 1938, ibid.; A.E. Armstrong to M.T.G. Mahon, 16 October 1939, ibid.
41. L.T. Yearwood to the governing body, 10 October 1940, ibid.
42. Ibid.
43. M.T.G. Mahon to A.E. Armstrong, 28 June 1938, ibid.
44. F.A. Collymore to M.T.G. Mahon, 4 May 1937; and M.T.G. Mahon to F.A. Collymore, 7 May 1937, ibid.
45. "Combermerians, Awake!", Gibbons Papers, II, n.p.
46. Governing body to the Education Board, 10 October 1936, Combermere School Records.
47. A.E. Armstrong to the governing body, 13 October 1937, ibid.
48. *Barbados Evening Advocate*, 18 February 1952; *Barbados Annual Review 1944*, 14, 22, 94; *Combermerian 1943-44*, 5; and *1944-45*, 19.
49. A.E. Armstrong to P.A.K. Tucker, 6 December 1943, Combermere School Records.
50. "Combermerians, Awake!", Gibbons Papers, II, n.p.
51. *Combermerian 1940-41*: 18.
52. Ibid., 4.
53. Ibid., 25-6; Thorn, passim. See also Sandiford, "The Contribution of Combermere school to the development of cricket in Barbados", *Cricket Lore* (forthcoming).
54. Gibbons Papers, II, n.p. See also A.E. Armstrong to the governing body, 4 February 1935, Combermere School Records.
55. M.T.G. Mahon to A.E. Armstrong, 22 July 1936, Combermere School Records
56. Combermere School Paysheets, 1934-46, ibid.; *Combermerian 1944-45*: 10.
57. Director of Education to the Secretary of the West India Committee, 31 January 1946, Combemere School Records..
58. Combermere School Paysheets, 1946, ibid.
59. *Combermere School Magazine*, December 1964: 12.
60. A.E. Armstrong to M.T.G. Mahon, 4 February 1935; and M.T.G. Mahon to A.E. Armstrong, 14 March 1935, ibid.
61. A.E. Armstrong to M.T.G. Mahon, 9 December 1937; and M.T.G. Mahon to A.E. Armstrong, 14 December 1937, ibid.
62. A.E. Armstrong to M.T.G. Mahon, 13 May 1941; and M.T.G. Mahon to A.E. Armstrong, 21 May 1941, ibid.
63. *Combermere School Magazine*, December 1964: 12.
64. *Combermerian 1938-39*.

CHAPTER FOUR

1. Howard Hayden to C.R. Stollmeyer, 1 March 1946 and 23 April 1946, Combermere School Records; the Director of Education to the Secretary, West India Committee, 31 January 1946, ibid.; C.R. Stollmeyer to Howard Hayden, 6 March 1946, ibid.; The governing body to C.R. Stollmeyer, 9 March 1946, ibid.; R. Gavin to Howard Hayden, 19 March 1946, ibid.; Howard Hayden to Major C. Noott, 23 April 1946, ibid.; The Director of Education to Major C. Noott, 24 April 1946, ibid.
2. Major Cecil Noott File, ibid.
3. Newspaper clipping, May 1946, ibid.; Salary Scales, Barbados 1945, ibid. See also F.A. Hoyos, *The Quiet Revolutionary* (London, 1984), 63.
4. Major C. Noott, "Memorandum re: School Organization", 11 October 1946, Combermere School Records.
5. Ibid.
6. The Prefects' Charter, ibid.
7. *Combermerian 1949-50*: 11-16.
8. Crichlow Challenge Cup, 1953-54, Combermere School Records.
9. J. Shoemaker and H. Fraser, "What Principals can do: some implications from studies of effective schooling", *Phi Delta Kappa*, (November 1981), 178-82.
10. Headmaster's Notes, 1947, Combermere School Records.
11. Ibid.
12. Ibid.
13. Headmaster's Address, 19 July 1950, 18, ibid.
14. Headmaster's Address, 21 March 1952, 16-17, ibid.
15. Headmaster's Address, 18 March 1953, 12-12, ibid.
16. Carl S. Herkes File, ibid.; Minutes of extraordinary governing body meeting, 8 November 1950, ibid.
17. Colin O'Kiersey File, ibid.
18. L.F. Emblem File, ibid.
19. Gibbons Papers, I, 67.
20. J.C.L. Drakes File, Combermere School Records
21. Major C. Noott to the acting Director of Education, 22 October 1957, ibid.
22. Major C. Noott, "Memorandum to the staff re: school organization, 1959", ibid.
23. Ibid.
24. Combermere School Examination Results, 1950-58, ibid.
25. E.g., Headmaster's Address, 19 July 1950, 10, ibid.
26. K.R. Broodhagen File, ibid. See also Gibbons Papers, I, 21-22.
27. James Millington interview, 4 October 1986.

28. J.A. Millington File, Combermere School Records. See also Major C. Noott to Miss M. Pindar, 2 April 1949, ibid.; "Minutes of the governing body meeting, 7 September 1954", ibid.
29. Headmaster's Address, 21 March 1952, 12, ibid.
30. D.E. Goddard File, ibid.
31. Headmaster's Address, 19 July 1950, 14-15, ibid. See also *Combermerian* 1944-45: 42.
32. Headmaster's Address, 21 March 1952, 11, Combermere School Records.
33. Report of a full inspection of Combermere School, February/March 1960, ibid.
34. Headmaster's Notes, 1947, 3, ibid.
35. Combermere School Receipts, 1948, ibid.
36. Minutes of governing body meeting, 6 November 1968, ibid.
37. *Barbados Annual Review 1944*, 117.
38. "Combermerians, Awake!", Gibbons Papers, II, n.p.
39. Headmaster's Address, 19 July 1950, 17.
40. Canteen Accounts, 1947-55, Combermere School Records.
41. Canteen Committee to governing body, 20 February 1959, ibid.; Minutes of governing body meeting, 28 May 1959, ibid.
42. Major C. Noott to P.A.K. Tucker, 11 June 1947, ibid.; Major C. Noott to Miss M. Pindar, 22 October 1948, ibid.
43. Ibid. See also Major C. Noott to the Director of Education, 3 October 1947, ibid.
44. Major C. Noott to the governing body, 28 March 1952, ibid.; Major C. Noott to Earle Newton, 10 February 1987.
45. Combermere School Scout Troop File, Combermere School Records.
46. Minutes of governing body meeting, 12 June 1951; Major C. Noott, Circular Letter to Parents, 28 June 1951; and Cave Shepherd & Co. Ltd. to Major C. Noott, 15 January 1952, ibid.
47. S.J. Adams File, ibid; Headmaster's Address, 21 March 1952, 13, ibid.
48. B.C. St John File, ibid.
49. H.G. Brewster File, ibid.
50. Major C. Noott, Memorandum re: Advanced Training at Combermere, 1951, ibid.
51. Miss M. Pindar to Major C. Glindon Reed, 22 February 1952; and Major C. Glindon Reed to Miss M. Pindar, 28 February 1952, ibid.
52. Minutes of governing body meeting, 7 September 1954, ibid.
53. V.B. Williams to the Director of Education, 23 June 1958, ibid.; Major C. Noott to the Director of Education, 16 March 1960, ibid.
54. Headmaster's Address, 20 March 1956, 7, ibid.

55. V.B. Williams to the Director of Education, 23 June 1958, ibid.
56. Major C. Noott to the Director of Education, 16 March 1960, ibid.
57. Combermere School Examination Results, 1954, ibid.
58. Combermere School Bills and Receipts, 1947-57, ibid.
59. Combermere School Magazine File, 1947-57, ibid.
60. Most of the governing body meetings in 1958 dealt with this thorny question of internal administration. See, especially, the Report of the Financial Committee, 4 July 1958, ibid.
61. Combermere School Paysheets, 1946-61, ibid.
62. Headmaster's Address, 20 March 1956, 6, ibid.
63. *Barbados Evening Advocate*, 18 February 1952.
64. See, e.g., A. Clegg and B. Megson, *Children in Distress* (New York, 1969).
65. Gibbons Papers, II, n.p.
66. Headmaster's Address, 20 March 1956, 1-3; and Reports on the Combermere School Buildings, 1949, Combermere School Records.
67. Headmaster's Address, 20 March 1956, ibid.
68. G.S.V. Petter, *Report of a Survey of Secondary Education in Barbados* (Bridgetown, 1956), passim.
69. F.E. Miller, "Provisional proposals for a scheme of reorganization, programme and policy of Combermere School", Combermere School Records.
70. Major C. Noott's comments on Miller's Provisional Proposals, ibid.
71. Governing body to the Director of Education, February 1956, ibid.
72. Headmaster's Address, 11 December 1959, 1-2, ibid.
73. S. Moffett et al., *Report of a Full Inspection of Combermere School*, February/March 1960 (Bridgetown, 1960).
74. Combermere Staff Observations re: Report of the General Inspection, 1960, Combermere School Records.
75. Combermere School Speech Day Programme, 16 March 1961, Combermere School Records.
76. Major C. Noott to the Director of Education, July 1957, ibid
77. Major C. Noott to the governing body, December 1957, ibid.
78. F.A. Collymore to Major Noott, 5 December 1957, ibid.
79. Minutes of the governing body meeting, 19 March 1958, ibid.
80. Combermere School bills and receipts, 1947-53, ibid.
81. Major C. Noott File, ibid.
82. Minutes of the governing body meeting, 7 September 1954, ibid.
83. A. Blumberg and W. Greenfield, *The Effective Principal: Perspectives on School Leadership* (Boston, 1980).
84. Major C. Noott File, Combermere School Records.

85. J.A. Millington interview, 4 October 1986.
86. Among several letters to the headmaster in March 1961, see especially Rev E.J. Pierce to Major C. Noott, 3 March 1961, Combermere School Records.
87. G.S.V. Petter, *Report 1956*, 23.
88. A. Douglas-Smith to Major C. Noott, 20 March 1956, Combermere School Records.
89. Ibid.
90. This item appears among several newspaper clippings left by Major Noott in the Combermere School Records. It is clear that he did not select only the positive pieces to leave for posterity. Although the majority are quite favourable, there are a few negative clippings as well.
91. These letters came from a wide range of pupils across the period of Noott's leadership. The writers included Ben Browne and Harold Crichlow (who taught at the school later on), Rudolph Knight and the Sealy twins, Philemon and Philip, among others.
92. Blumberg and Greenfield, viii.
93. Hoyos, *From Amerindians to Independence*, 217-26.
94. Beckles, *From Amerindian Settlement to Nation State*, 189-93
95. See the *Barbados Colonial Estimates* for the period 1940-58 and the *Barbados Estimates* for the years 1959-61.
96. *Barbados Colonial Estimates 1949-50*, 38; *Barbados Colonial Estimates 1959-60*, 42.

CHAPTER FIVE

1. *Combermere School Magazine*, Second Term 1923-24: 5; *Combermerian 1943-44*: 6; *Harrisonian*, December 1931: 53; April 1944: 5; and December 1944: 7; *Barbados Annual Review 1944*: 22, 59.
2. Hamilton: 139, 141, 150, 154-7; Thorn: 11, 24.
3. *Combermere School Magazine*, December 1964: 8.
4. Ibid.
5. Minutes of governing body meetings, 19 September and 6 November 1968, and of 25 March and 2, 7 & 17 May 1969, Combermere School Records.
6. K.C. Jacobs, *Education Commission Report* (Bridgetown, 1961), passim.
7. See Combermere School Paysheets, 1970-79, Combermere School Records.
8. *Combermere School Magazine*, December 1964: 8-11.
9. Ibid., 8.
10. Ibid.
11. Minutes of governing body meeting, 12 January 1970, Combermere School Records; C.B. Best File, ibid.

12. *Combermere School Magazine*, December 1964: 8.
13. Combermere School Examination Reports, 1960-71, Combermere School Records.
14. S. O'C. Gittens to the Director of Music, Royal Barbados Police Band, 27 February 1969, ibid.
15. *Combermere School Magazine*, December 1964: 10-11.
16. Headmaster's rough notes, 1973?, Combermere School Records.
17. S. O'C. Gittens to the governing body, 12 September 1963, ibid.; Combermere School Paysheets, October & November 1956, ibid.; P.A.F. Branch File, ibid.
18. Personal interviews with Ronald Bruce and Keith Sandiford, 1986-91; Keith Albert Sandiford to Keith A.P. Sandiford, 26 March 1990.
19. Minutes of governing body meeting, 5 November 1953, Combermere School Records.
20. C. DeV. Moore File, ibid.
21. Ibid.
22. Combermere School Staff List, 1977-78, ibid.
23. Headmaster's Notes, 1979, ibid. Combermere School Paysheets, September 1946 to December 1961, ibid. Combermere School Draft Estimates, 1961-71, ibid. Barbados, *Report of the Department of Education for the Year Ended 31 March 1947*, 22; Ministry of Education, *Report from 1 January 1970 to 31 August 1971*, 18-19.
24. Interview with Charles W. Pilgrim, 10 October 1986; Minutes of governing body meeting, 15 June 1976, Combermere School Records; Headmaster's Business, governing body meeting, 30 June 1977, ibid.; Headmaster's Business, Board of Management meeting, 22 June 1983, ibid.
25. Interview with Charles W. Pilgrim, 10 October 1986; Combermere School Cadet Company Report, 1973-74, Combermere School Records.
26. Headmaster's Notes, 1979, Combermere School Records; Combermere School Staff, 1982-83, ibid.
27. Agenda for governing body meeting, 8 January 1973, ibid.; Headmaster's Business, governing body meeting, 27 February 1973, ibid.
28. Minutes of governing body meeting, 12 September 1968, ibid.
29. Headmaster's Business, governing body meeting, 30 June 1977, ibid.
30. Scoutmaster's Notice, 2 March 1962, ibid.
31. Patrick Skeete to governing body, 27 October 1980, ibid.
32. Combermere School Games Report, 1973-74, ibid. Minutes of governing body meeting, 9 August 1979, ibid.
33. Combermere School Report, 1973-74, ibid.
34. Barbados Cricket Association, *Report and Statement of Accounts from 1 April 1976 to 31 March 1977*, 6.

35. Combermere School Games Report, 1973-74, Combermere School Records.
36. The Prefects' Charter, 1964-65, ibid.
37. Combermere School Set Organization, 1970-71, ibid.
38. Combermere School, Draft Estimates, 1976-77, ibid.
39. Combermere School Examination Reports, 1977-81, ibid.
40. Ibid.
41. Combermere School Staff List, 1977-78, ibid.
42. C. DeV. Moore File, ibid.
43. Minutes of Board of Management meeting, 21 May 1985, ibid.
44. *Barbados Estimates 1963-64*, viii, ix; and *1982-83*, i, 9. See also Sandiford, "Education and the Barbadian society".

CHAPTER SIX

1. *Harrisonian*, July 1950, 1.
2. Agenda for Staff Meeting, 18 April 1977, Combermere School Records.
3. Interview with Charles W. Pilgrim, 10 October 1986.
4. Reports of Sub-Committees to the Board of Management Chairperson, 14 March 1984, Combermere School Records.
5. Examination Reports, 1970-86, ibid.
6. Reports on GCE Examination Results, Summer 1981, ibid.
7. GCE Examination Report, Summer 1982, ibid; Minutes of governing body meeting, 18 November 1982, ibid.
8. Combermere School Staff to Major C. Noott, 29 June 1959, ibid.
9. Examination Reports, 1983-87, ibid. See also Ralph Boyce to all head teachers, 14 November 1982, ibid.
10. Ministry of Education to the governing body, 23 July 1981, ibid.
11. Minutes of governing body meeting, 17 August 1981, ibid.
12. W.A. Burke to Mrs M.M. Rudder, 24 July 1981 and 24 September 1982, ibid.; Mrs M.M. Rudder to W.A. Burke, 20 October 1981 and 17 November 1982, ibid.; K. Inniss to Mrs M.M. Rudder, 14 May 1982, ibid.; Minutes of governing body meeting, 17 August 1981, and 5 August 1982, ibid.
13. Ministry of Education to governing body, 23 August 1982, ibid. Minutes of governing body meeting, 16 November 1982 and 3 March 1983, ibid.
14. Minutes of emergency governing body meeting with Combermere Staff, 2 February 1984, ibid.
15. Ibid.
16. Minutes of governing body meeting, 21 April 1983, ibid.
17. Agenda, Combermere School Staff meeting, 3 January 1983, ibid.

18. Minutes of Board of Management meeting, 22 June 1983, ibid.
19. Minutes of Board of Management meeting, 9 September 1983, ibid.
20. Minutes of Emergency Board of Management meeting with the Combermere School Staff, 2 February 1984, ibid.
21. Minutes of Emergency Board of Management meeting, 19 January 1984, ibid.
22. Minutes of Board of Management meeting, 22 May 1984, ibid.; Ministry of Education to Charles W. Pilgrim, 11 May 1984, and Charles W. Pilgrim to Ministry of Education, 17 May 1984, ibid.
23. Reports of Sub-Committees to the Board of Management Chairperson, 14 March 1984, ibid.
24. Minutes of Board of Management meeting, 24 January 1985, ibid.
25. Combermere School Estimates of Expenditure, 1946-51, ibid.
26. Estimates of Expenditure, 1959-61, ibid.
27. Combermere School Draft Estimates, 1974-76, ibid.
28. Draft Estimates, 1986-90, ibid.
29. Marcia Millward to K.A.P. Sandiford, 9 March 1990.
30. Interviews with Charles W. Pilgrim and Keith A. Roach, October 1986.
31. Sandiford, "Education and the Barbadian Society".

CHAPTER SEVEN

1. "Combermerians, Awake!", Gibbons Papers, II, n.p.
2. Similar remarks were made by Barrow when he delivered the eulogy at St Hill's funeral in August 1985.
3. After the demise of the West Indian Federation following the withdrawal of Jamaica and Trinidad & Tobago, efforts were made to keep the remaining eight territories together. When the then premier, Errol Barrow, decided he had had enough of negotiating because no progress was being made and that he would take Barbados into independence, Crawford resigned his portfolio and left the DLP. He was a devoted believer in West Indian unity and felt that greater efforts should continue in order to insure the unification of the so-called Little Eight.
4. *Bajan*, January 1973: 12-31.
5. Victor Isaac and Philip Thorn, *Hampshire Cricketers 1800-1982* (Nottingham, 1983), 11, 31. See also Sandiford, "The role of Combermere School in the development of cricket in Barbados", *Cricket Lore* (forthcoming).
6. Major C. Noott File, Combermere School Records.; Major C. Noott to K.A.P. Sandiford, 7 September 1986.; Sandiford and Stoddart, 333-50.
7. Personal interviews, June-October 1986, with Barbadians who had attended secondary schools during the 1950s. This cross-section included Nigel

Bradshaw (Lodge), Clyde King (Foundation), Andrew Lewis (Combermere), Grace Pilgrim (Queen's College), Gregg Rowe (Harrison College), Alfred St John (Coleridge Parry) and Calvin Yarde (Harrison College).
8. Harold Marshall to K.A.P. Sandiford, 15 February 1987.

SELECT BIBLIOGRAPHY

PRIMARY SOURCES

Collymore (Frank) Private Papers, Department of Archives, Barbados.
Combermere School Annual Audits.
Combermere School Estimates and Draft Estimates of Annual Expenditures.
Combermere School Records, Waterford.
Frank L. Gibbons Private Papers.
Personal Interviews.
Recopied Deeds, Department of Archives, Barbados.
Recopied Wills, Department of Archives, Barbados.

MAGAZINES, NEWSPAPERS AND PERIODICALS

Advocate Year Book and Who's Who. Advocate Co. Ltd 1951, 1964
Bajan & South Caribbean. Carib Publicity Co. 1953-1981
Barbados Advocate 1895 to date
Barbados Agricultural Reporter 1870-1910
Barbados Annual Review Barbados Stomara Publicity Co. 1942-1955
Barbados Nation Nation Publishing Co. 1973 to date.
Combermere School Magazine, 1913-1925
Combermerian, 1926-1974
Harrisonian, 1903-1993
Journal of the Barbados Museum and Historical Society. Garrison, St Michael. The Society. Vols. 1-3
Lodge School Record, 1911-1993
New Bajan. Nation Publishing Co. 1987-1992

Select Bibliography

PUBLIC DOCUMENTS

Barbados. Commission on Education Report 1875. John Michinson (Chairman), 1875

Barbados. Education Act 1890

Barbados. Commission on Education Report 1894-96 (Bridgetown, 1896)

Barbados. Education Commission Report 1907-09 (Bridgetown, 1909)

Barbados. Education Act 1981

Barbados. Barbados Estimates (Bridgetown, 1898-1992)

Barbados, House of Assembly. Legislative Debates 1884 to date

Board of Education. Education in Barbados: Statistical and Other Information (Bridgetown, 1931)

Board of Education. Special Reports on Educational Subjects (London, 1968)

Colonial Annual Reports on Barbados 1929-1963. London: HMSO. 1929-57 & Barbados Government Printing Office 1958-1963

Colony of Barbados. Blue Books. 1833-1947

Jacobs, K.C. Commission Report 1961. Report of Commission Appointed to Review Structure of the Civil Service. (Barbados, 1961)

Laws of Barbados

Miller, F.E. Provisional Proposals for a Scheme of Reorganization, Programme and Policy of Combermere School (1957)

Ministry of Education. Report on External Examination Results 1970

Ministry of Education. Annual Reports. 1910-1982

Petter, G.S.V. Report of a Survey of Secondary Education in Barbados (Bridgetown, 1956)

Went, T.E. et al. Report on Combermere School Buildings (Bridgetown, 1949)

West India Royal Commission. Notes on the System of Education in Barbados (London, 1939)

SECONDARY SOURCES

Beckles, H. McD. 1990. *A History of Barbados: From Amerindian Settlement to Nation State*. Cambridge.

Bennis, W., & B Nanus. 1985. *Leaders: the Strategies for Taking Charge*. New York.

Bindley, T.H. N.d. *Annals of Codrington College Barbados 1710-1910*. London.

Blumberg A., & W. Greenfield. 1980. *The Effective Principal: Perspectives on School Leadership*. Boston.

Burns, J.M. 1978. *Leadership*. New York.

Clegg, A., & B. Megson. 1969. *Children in Distress*. New York.

Doll, D.C. 1969. *Variations Among Inner City Elementary Schools.* Kansas.
Dyson, A.E., and J. Lovelock, eds. 1975. *Education and Democracy.* London.
Evans, R.J., ed. *1978. Social Policy 1830-1914: Industrialization, Collectivism and the Origins of the Welfare State.* London.
Figueroa, J. 1971. *Society, Schools and Progress in the West Indies.* Oxford.
Goldhammer, K., et al. 1971. *Elementary Principals and Their Schools: Beacons of Brilliance and Potholes of Pestilence.* Oregon.
Gordon, S.C. 1963. *A History of West Indian Education.* London.
―――― 1968. Reports and Repercussions in West Indian Education 1835-1933. London.
Greenhalgh, N. 1927. "Education in Barbados". *Barbados Diocesan History*, edited by J.E. Reece and C.G. Clark-Hunt. London.
Gross, N., and R.E. Herriott. 1965. *Staff Leadership in Public Schools: A Sociological Enquiry.* New York.
Hamilton, B. 1947. *Cricket in Barbados.* Bridgetown.
Hayden, H. 1943. *The Purpose of Education.* Bridgetown.
―――― 1945. *A Policy for Education.* Bridgetown.
―――― 1945. "Education in Barbados", *Empire Digest*, April: 41-44.
Heyck, T.W. 1992. *The Peoples of the British Isles: From 1870 to the Present.* California.
Hoyos, F.A. 1945. *Two Hundred Years: A History of the Lodge School.* Bridgetown.
―――― 1988. *Barbados: A History from the Amerindians to Independence.* London.
―――― 1984. *The Quiet Revolutionary.* London.
Hurt, J.S. 1979. *Elementary Schooling and the Working Classes 1860-1918.* London.
Isaac V., & P. Thorn. 1983. *Hampshire Cricketers 1800-1982.* Nottingham.
Jarman, T.L. 1963. *Landmarks in the History of Education.* London.
Lane, J., ed. *Management Techniques for School Districts Reston Vancouver.*
Lowenthal, D. 1967. "Race and colour in the West Indies". *Daedalus: Journal of the American Academy of Arts and Sciences 96* (Spring): 580-626.
―――― 1972. *West Indian Societies.* London.
Lynch, L.A. 1964. *The Barbados Book.* London.
Monroe, P. 1924. *A Brief Course in the History of Education.* London.
Newton, E.H., & K.A.P. Sandiford. 1988. "A study in the administrative technique of an effective headmaster: Combermere School under Major Cecil Noott, 1946-61". *Bulletin of Eastern Caribbean Affairs* 14 (March-June): 41-57.
Reader, W.J. 1964. *Life in Victorian England.* London.
Reece, J.E., & C.G. Clark-Hunt, eds. 1927. *Barbados Diocesan History.* London.
Roebuck, J.A. 1974. *The Making of Modern English Society From 1850.* Newton Abbot.

Sandiford, K.A.P. 1986. "Cricket and the Barbadian society". *Canadian Journal of History* 21 (December): 353-70.

———— 1987. "Combermere School and the Barbadian society". *Caribe* (April): 12-14.

———— 1988. "Combermere School, 1926-46: twenty years of rapid growth". *Banja: A Magazine of Barbadian Life & Culture* (August): 44-53.

———— 1989. "Education and the Barbadian Society". *Banja: A Magazine of Barbadian Life & Culture* (April): 45-53.

———— 1989. "Combermere School under G.B.R. Burton (1897-1925)". *Journal of Caribbean Studies* 7 (Spring): 99-113.

———— & B. Stoddart. 1987. "The Elite schools and cricket in Barbados: A study in colonial continuity". *The International Journal of the History of Sport* 4 (December): 333-70.

Shoemaker, J., & H. Fraser. 1981. "What principals can do: some implications from studies of effective schooling". *Phi Delta Kappa* (November): 178-82.

Starratt, J. 1986. *Excellence in Education and Quality of Leadership*. Geelong.

Thorn, P. 1991. *Barbados Cricketers 1865-1990*. Nottingham.

Williams, E. 1969. *Education in the British West Indies*. New York.

Woodward, E.L. 1962. *The Age of Reform: 1815-70*. Oxford.

THESES AND SEMINAR PAPERS

Gibbs, B. 1977. "Government and the problem of social reconstruction, 1838-49". Seminar paper no. 3, 1976-77, UWI, Cave Hill.

Gilmore, J. 1982. "Serving two masters: religious literature in Barbados, c. 1780 to 1834". Seminar paper no. 1, 1982-83, UWI, Cave Hill.

———— 1984. "Episcopacy, emancipation, and evangelization". Seminar paper no. 6, 1983-84, UWI, Cave Hill.

Goodridge, R.V. 1966. "The development of education in Barbados, 1818-1860". MEd thesis, University of Leeds.

Karch, C. 1983. "London Bourne of Barbados". Paper presented at the Fifteenth Conference of Caribbean Historians, UWI, Mona, (April).

Layne, A. 1976. "Education and social change in Barbados". PhD diss., University of Calgary.

Layne, D. 1976. "Politics and education expansion in Barbados". MA thesis, University of Calgary.

Leslie, S. 1984. "Education for girls in Barbados in 1850". Seminar paper no. 8, 1983-84, UWI, Cave Hill.

Phillips, A. DeV. n.d. "The racial factor in politics in Barbados 1880-1914". Seminar paper, UWI, Cave Hill.

Titus, N. 1982. "Methodism and social change in Barbados, 1838-1883: an overview". Seminar paper no. 6, 1981-82, UWI, Cave Hill.

Vaughan, H.A. 1982. "The shaping of the new order: Barbados 1834-46". Seminar paper no. 9, 1981-82, UWI, Cave Hill.

Williams, A.G. 1964. "The development of education in Barbados with special reference to social and economic conditions 1834-1958". MA thesis, University of London.

INDEX

Aberystwyth 69
Abolitionists 2
Adams, Sir Grantley 101, 121
Adams, J.M.G.M. 'Tom' 121
Adams, S. Jack 73, 85
Advocate Year Book and Who's Who 1951 34
Alexandra Girls' School 28, 29
Alkins, H.F. Bert 49, 65
Alkins, Peter 117
Allen, Mr 4
Alleyne, Charles G. 63, 147
Alleyne, Ezra 116
Alleyne, Sir John Gay 6
Alleyne School 14, 28, 29, 52, 68
Alliance Française de la Barbade 97
Anglican Church 6, 86
Anglo-Boer War 41
Antigua 48
Apprenticeship system 9
Archer, C.V.H. 38, 45
Archer, David 143
Armstrong, Rev Arthur Evelyn 55-68, 69, 71, 72, 73, 75, 78, 80, 90, 102, 103, 108, 110, 114, 116, 134, 137, 144
Armstrong, George Leslie 156
Armstrong Memorial Prize 67, 116
Armstrong Private School 55
Armstrong Scholarships 52
Arrindell, Hugh 34, 39
Atkins, Professor Cyril 45
Atkinson, Denis 8, 143
Atkinson, Eric 8, 143
Atkinson, W. St Eval 8
Austin, Sir Harold B.G. 51-52, 53,

Balfour, A.J. 7
Banfield, Col Leonard 142
Barbados Advocate 25, 26, 27, 36, 89, 91, 99
Barbados Agricultural Reporter 29, 31, 36
Barbados Cadet Battalion 39
Barbados Community College 104, 105
Barbados Cricket Association 104
Barbados Defence Force 142
Barbados Labour Party 64, 101, 121
Barbados Lumber Company 143
Barbados Observer 64, 140
Barbados Regiment 142
Barbados Scholarship 13, 19, 88, 111, 124, 126
Barbados SPCK 4, 6, 8
Barbados Volunteer Force 39
Barbados Workers' Union 64
Barclay, Anthony 18
Barker, R. Hugh 124
Barnsley 69
Barrett, A.L. 119
Barrow, Errol Walton 14, 45, 101, 105, 121, 131, 139, 164
Barrow, Everton 125
Barrow, Dame Nita 45
Barrow, Rev Reginald 45
Batson, C.S. 34
Batson, Richard E. 34, 35
Battle of Britain 71
Bayne, Henry D. 34, 39
Beckles, H.A.M. 37, 38, 45
Bedford, E. 15
Belgrave, George 116, 129, 131, 147
Bell, Gordon O. 67, 73, 89

171

Bell, Sarah Jane 23
Bell, Sir Philip 23
Belle, Orville 142
Belleville 15
Belper 71
Berger Paints Ltd 143
Beryl 82
Best, Clyde B. 'Charlie' 94, 106
Bim 143
Birkett, Lionel S. 41
Bishop, Frank 45
Blackman, Mrs Gloria 116
Blackman, Harold 140
Blenman, Dr E.H. Morris 147
Blumberg, A. 100
Bob-a-Job Week 83
Bond, Hon Francis 3
Bookstore, 65, 80, 81, 105
Bourne, Lincoln 18
Bowen, the porter 136
Bowen, E.G. 33
Boxill, Charles 126
Boxing 86
Boyce, Ralph 126
Bradshaw, Nigel 146, 164-165
Branch, Phil A.F. 110
Branch, Rev S.F. 10
Brancker & Company 143
Brancker, Rawle 85, 100, 143
Brathwaite, Chris 45, 46, 140
Brathwaite, G. Ralph 67, 81, 84, 105
Brathwaite, John 8, 9
Brathwaite, Melanie 126
Brathwaite, Roderick 126
Bree, Bishop 17
Bree Commission 17
Brewster, Harold Gittens 62, 65, 86, 117, 145
Bridgetown 1, 2, 33, 36, 81, 103, 143
British Council 83
British Commonwealth 100
British Empire 39, 41, 45, 100
British Guiana 48, 78
British Virgin Islands 131
Broodhagen, Karl 78, 86, 92, 98, 116, 128, 142
Broodhagen, Virgil 78
Brooker, Dudley DeC 67
Browne, Elon Benoni 111, 119, 146, 161
Browne, Cyril R. 'Snuffie' 143
Bruce, Ronald Ainsley 111
Bryan, T.O. 34, 45

Bulkeley, Rowland 6
Bullard, Benjamin 3
Burke, Walter 127, 142
Burma 69, 71, 145
Burton, G.B.R. 23-47, 48, 49, 50, 51, 54, 57, 63, 65, 68, 72, 103, 107, 111, 114, 143, 144
Burton, George James 23
Burton, Norah 46
Bush, Hall 113
Bushe, Sir Henry Grattan 60

Callender, Blyden 114
Callender, Victor 85
Cambridge School Certificate 27, 36, 37, 38, 40, 50, 54, 65, 66, 74, 80, 87, 88
Campbell, Douglas 114
Canada 69, 78, 146, 147
Canteen 65, 81-82
Canteen Subcommittee 82
Carew, George 143
Caribbean Examination Council 119-120, 134-135
Carifta Games 117
Carrington, John 3
Carter, William H. 35, 39, 40, 45, 49, 51
Cave Shepherd & Co. Ltd. 84
Cawthorne, J.P. 10
Central Boys' School 3-4, 6-13, 15, 23
Central Girls' School 7, 13
Central Middle School 9
Central Schools' Act, (1859) 13
Centre Linguistique 147
Ceylon 71
Chaderton, J.E. 15, 33
Chase, Major A. DeV. 45
Chase, Errol 142, 147
Chenery, J.W.B. 38, 45
Chenery, Percy 129
Christ Church 11
Clarke, Austin A.C. 143
Clarke, Dr Belfield 45
Clarke, Dr Carl 140
Clarke, Rev Charles 14
Clarke, Dr Desmond 142, 147
Clarke, George 4
Clarke, H.W. 58
Clarke, Rev Thomas 10
Clement, the porter 136
Clinkett, R.J. 27
Codrington, Christopher 2, 3, 6

Index

Codrington College 23, 33, 34, 48, 55, 103, 112, 114
Coke College, Antigua 48
Coleridge, Bishop William Hart 6, 22
Coleridge School 14, 24, 25, 26, 28, 52, 68
Coleridge-Parry School 146
Collymore, Frank Appleton 35, 36, 39, 40, 42, 45, 49, 50, 54, 57, 59, 65, 67, 75, 80, 95, 98, 142-143, 146, 147
Collymore, Samuel Francis 18
Colonial Charity School 3
Colonial Office 18, 30
Combermere Alumni Association (USA) 46, 116, 139
Combermere, Lord 4, 6, 13
Combermere Mutual Improvement Association 42, 116
Combermere School Cadet Band 117, 130
Combermere School Cadet Company 39, 83, 92, 107, 110, 116, 117, 124, 130
Combermere School Library 80-81, 105
Combermere School Literary & Debating Society 108, 124
Combermere School Magazine 39, 42, 107
Combermere School Old Boys' Association 42, 67, 97, 116
Combermere School Old Scholars' Association 42, 99, 100, 117, 124, 133, 136, 139, 146
Combermere School Parent Teachers' Association 124
Combermere School Photographic Club 123
Combermere School Scout Troop 39, 49, 84, 92, 105, 107, 117, 124
Combermere School Song 84, 133
Combermerian 42, 49, 89
Common Entrance Examinations 117, 124, 125, 137
Commonwealth 1
Constitution Hill 3, 7, 13, 41, 53, 60-61, 64, 68, 82
Coppin, C.A. 97
Corbin, C.F.A. 35, 36, 37, 49, 65, 146
Corbin, Mrs Effie Jane 61
Corbin, Samuel 142
Cordle, E. 33
Coronation Pageant 97
'Cow Shed' 58, 59, 82
Cox, G.B.Y. 'Gussie' 48-55, 57, 61, 65, 68, 72, 102, 104, 114, 144

Cox, Mencea 121
Crawford, Wynter 45, 64, 121, 140, 164
Crichlow Challenge Cup 73
Crichlow, Rev Harold E. 73, 83, 87, 142, 161
Crick, Cuthbert O'Brien 63
Cricket 22, 40, 41-42, 48, 49, 53, 57, 62-64, 85-86, 104, 107, 117, 135, 143
Croydon 147
Cummins, Thomas 18

Dalton Cup 107
Dash, Professor J. Sydney 45
Davies, E.B. 97, 104, 107
Davies, Mrs 104
Davis, Woodbine 142
Deane, L.E. 33
Dear, Cyril 15, 33
Deighton, Horace 14, 16, 22, 23, 41, 49, 55
Democratic Labour Party 86, 101, 113, 121, 140, 164
Department of National Archives 83
Department of Science & Agriculture 17
Depradine, Colin 126
Devonish, C. 51
Doorly, M.E. 15
Douglas-Smith, Aubrey 98
Downes, Dr Andrew 142
Downie, Rev Casper 34
Drakes, J. Cleophas D 65, 67, 77
Drax, Col Henry 1, 2, 3, 6, 42
Drax, Sir James 1
Drax Free School 2-3
Drax Hall Estate 1
Drax Parish School 3-4
Drill Hall, Garrison 73, 90, 91-92, 95
Dryher, Mr 4
Durant, Orville 142
Durham University 114

Education Act (1822) 6, 19
Education Act (1846) 19
Education Act (1850) 19
Education Act (1878) 11, 14, 19, 22
Education Act (1890) 11, 19, 26, 28
Education Act (1897) 19
Education Act (1981) 97, 123-124, 127, 128, 129, 130-131
Education Board 19, 59, 82, 83, 87, 90, 96, 114
Education Committee 19

Education, Ministry of 20, 100, 105, 115, 118, 124, 126-133
Edwards, Gregg O. 147
Ellerslie Secondary School 129
Ellis, Robert 10
Elliott, R.P. 9, 22
Emancipation 9, 18, 19
Emblem, L.F. 77
Empire Cricket Club 104
Emtage, Oliver DeCourcey 26, 27
English Charitable Society 7
Erdiston College 94
Escoffery, Gloria 116
Europe 71
Evans, T.L. 145
Eversley 146

Farnum, P.R. 15
Farmer, Hon John 3
Farmer, W.A. 71
Ferguson, George 45, 140
Field hockey 85, 92, 117, 135
First World War 34, 41, 43, 45
Fletcher, Dr John 106, 111
Foderingham, C. 15, 33
Football (soccer) 40, 41, 42, 104, 107, 117
Forde C.B. 62
Forde, Woodbine 29, 33
Foundation Boys' School 35, 49, 52, 68, 124, 146
Foundation School Old Scholars' Associations 146
Frank Collymore Hall 80
Franklin, A.B. 53
Franklin, Warwick 140
Free School 3

Gallop, Samuel 4
Games Fund 66, 83
Garrison Secondary School 129
Genders, Rev 112
Germans 45
Germany 69
Gibbons, Frank Leo 37, 38, 46, 47, 49, 50, 51, 57, 61, 65, 85, 90, 91, 139, 140, 155
Gibbs, Bentley 151
Gibbs, Cuthbert Lisle 34
Gibbs, Hon John 3
Gibson, Irwin 126
Giles, C.H. 15, 33

Gilkes, Benjamin I. 41
Gill, George 4
Gill, Ossie 85
Girls' Industrial Union 58
Gittens, Lionel Lester 63, 67, 75, 82, 103, 108, 127, 128
Gittens, L.O. 103, 107
Gittens, Stanton O'Connor 63, 65, 95, 103-113, 114, 117, 121, 122, 123, 133, 134
Glee Club 79
Glindon Reed, Major C. 87
Globe Theatre 97
Goddard, Dennis E. 67, 80, 95, 146
Goddard, H.L. 65
Goldsmith College of Art 79
Goodman, Aubrey 28
Goring, Livingstone F. 83, 88, 94, 106
Government Industrial Schools 17
'Grannie' 82
Grayfoot Mrs 8
Great Britain 1, 6-7, 9, 12, 14, 18, 20, 44, 77
Green Hill 113
Greenfield, W. 100
Greenidge, J.A. 10
Greenidge, Rev N.H. 17
Gregory, Mrs Jacqueline 100
Grenada Grammar School 103
Griffith, Herman 41, 143
Griffiths, R.F. 41
Guy, Richard 3

Hamlet, Dr H.I. 45
Hall, Burton 35, 49
Hall, Capt Radcliffe R. 39
Hall, Wesley Winfield 85, 100, 140, 143, 147
Hall's Road 85
Harbin, J.A. 15
Harewood, Dr Stephen 142
Harris, Edward 4
Harris, Thomas 18
Harrison College 4, 8, 11, 12, 13, 14, 16, 22, 23, 26, 27, 29, 35, 37, 38, 39, 42, 48, 52, 53, 55, 58, 69, 85, 87, 98, 102, 103, 104, 112, 113, 124, 134, 137, 140, 144, 145, 146
Harrison Free School 4, 8, 9
Haskell, Harold Noad 53
Haverfordwest 95
Haverfordwest Grammar School 69

Index

Hayden, Howard 69
Haynes, Trevor 85
Headley, the porter 136
Headley, Sam 145
Herald 64
Herbert Strutt School 71
Herkes, Carl S. 76
Hernaman, A.F. 17, 23, 25
Hill, T.C. 77
Hinds, A.A. 38
Hoad, E.L.G. Snr 41, 143
Holder, Elsworth St. A. 45, 140
Holder, John 143
Holder, Gilbert 85
Holder, Gladstone A. 65, 67, 73, 81, 98, 146
Holder, Kenneth 147
Holder, Ralph 117
Holgate Grammar School 69
Hope Plantation 23
Hope, J. Chamberlain 47
Hothersall, John 3
House of Assembly 27, 28, 101, 140
House system (sets) 20, 40-41, 50, 67, 72-74, 92, 111, 118
Howard, J.I.C. 33
Howard, Dr Michael 142
Howe, Hon William 3
Hoyos, 'Fab' 65, 71, 149
Hudson, Gerald 66, 79, 106
Hughes, Ronald G. 78, 85-86
Hull, Rev James 4
Hunte, G.B. 65
Hunte, Grace 90
Hunte, Dr Reginald 45
Hunte, St. Clair 34, 143
Husbands, K.N.R. 101
Hutchinson, Harold G. 3, 35, 49, 65, 66, 149
Hutchinson, Leo R. 34, 35, 41, 46

Ince, Carl Leon 85
India 71, 145
Indian River 3
Industrial Arts 106, 125
Infants' Central School 6, 13
Inniss, Errie 85
Inspector of Schools 9, 19
Island Scholarships 13, 19, 23, 26, 38, 48, 55
Island Scout Council 83
Ishmael, Alan F. 63

Jacobs Commission (1961) 105
Jamaica 77, 164
Jean-Marie, David 126, 130
Jebodsingh, Annette 135
Jordan, Jean 119

Kennedy, Joseph 18
Kensington Oval 41, 48
Kidney, John McColl 40, 46
King, Clyde M. 165
King, Frank 85
King, H.C. 20
King, Horace 129
King, Keith 114
King's Flag 39
Knight, Rudolph 161
Knight, Vernon 34, 143

Laborde, Edward 30, 34
Lamming, George 143
Larrier, Lola 119
Lashley, Patrick 'Peter' 85, 100, 143
Laurie, G.F. 10
Layne, Rev 112
Layne, Clarrie 119
Layne, Edward 142
Learmond, George 22
Lewis, Andrew 142, 165
Lewis, Harcourt 140
Lillington, Hon George 3
Little Eight 140, 164
Lobo, Evan 34
Lodge School, the 8, 11, 12, 13, 18, 20, 22, 23, 26, 27, 29, 33, 39, 49, 52, 58, 71, 78, 85, 87, 102, 104, 110, 112, 114, 124, 140, 144, 145, 146
'Lodge School Parent' 99
London 1, 65, 81, 146
London Chamber of Commerce Examinations 27, 36, 50, 54, 63, 74, 88
London GCE 88
London University 94
Loughborough College 86
Louisiana State University 111, 147
Lucas, John Herman 63
Lynch, James A. 18

Mahon, M.T.G. 59, 90
Major Noott Hall 100
Maloney, Mrs 82
Mandeville, Rev A.F. 34
Manitoba 146, 147

Marian Anderson Concert 97
Marshall, Harold 143, 146
Martindale, E.A. 'Mannie' 55, 143
Massiah, W.H.B. 15
Mayers, Janice 119
Maynard, Lt Col Deighton 83, 85, 117, 142, 146
Maynard, Frank A. 147
McKenzie, R.B. 34
McLean, Wendell 116, 142
Measuring the Moment 147
Medford, Gordon 129
'Medicus' 26
Michinson, Bishop John 10, 22
Michinson Commission 11-14, 19
Miller, Fred 93, 140, 143, 147
Millington, James A. 79-80, 92, 97, 98, 106, 111, 128, 142
Mittelholtzer, Edgar 143
Missionaries 2
Moffett, Stanley 94
Moore, C. DeVere 89, 105, 108, 109, 114-121, 122, 123, 127, 133
Moore, Colin A. 67
Moore, Rev Henry W. 10, 15, 23
Mottley, J. 125
Mundy, Governor Robert 10
Murray, Glynne 116

Newsam, A.R.V. 71
Newsam, Sir Frank 45
Newton, Cammie 85
Newton, Professor Earle H. 73, 88, 142
Newton, Samuel 3
New York 83, 106
Nicholls, Dr Winston 147
Noott, Major Cecil 68, 69-102, 103, 104, 106, 107, 108, 111, 113, 114, 115, 116, 118, 121, 122, 125, 127, 128, 130, 138, 139, 142, 144, 145, 147, 161
Noott, Mrs Kathleen 100

Odell, John 4
O'Kiersey, Colin 77
Ottawa 147
Owen, Michael 104
Oxford & Cambridge Examinations 88, 111, 120

Packer, Hon Charles 10
Parochial Charity School 3
Panama 46-47

Parravicino, R. 33
Parry Rev H.H. 10
Parry School 14, 17, 24, 25, 28, 68
Payne, Dame Elsie 105
Payne, John N. 119
Peck, George Edgar 91
Peers, George 3
Pembrokeshire 69
Perking, Dudley Ralph 67, 83, 146
Peter-Newlands, Monica 135
Petter Report (1956) 93
Petter, G.V.S. 93, 97
Phillips, Amory 140, 143
Phillips, Anthony DeV 151
Phillips, Cedric 114
Phillips, John Hartley 4
Phipps, Charles 18
Pickwick Cricket Club 55
Pierce, Rev E.J. 97
Pile, Colvin 146
Pile, Dorien 119, 134, 135
Pile, Kenneth 142
Pilgrim, Charles W. 83, 107, 108, 114, 118, 122-133, 134, 137, 138, 146
Pilgrim, Grace 146, 165
Pilgrim, Owen Alexander 'Graffie' 49, 50, 55, 57, 65, 79
Pilgrim, Sheila 129, 130
Pilgrim, Torrey 145
'Pilgrim's Place' 11
'Pin' 26
Pindar, Miriam Naomi 90
Pitt, William 147
Prefect's Charter 72, 118
Prefect system 40-41, 50, 67, 73, 93, 112, 118
Prescod, Samuel Jackman 18
Price, Alfred B. 29, 33
Professional Development Day 128
Public Library 17, 81

Queen's College 3, 7, 12, 13, 14, 29, 52, 60, 61, 102, 105, 124, 146
Queen's Park 41, 91
Queen's Royal College 145

Ramsay, J.T.C. 58
Rawle, Richard 19
Rawson, Governor Rawson W. 10
Reece, A. 33
Reece, H.W. 28
Reeves, Sir Conrad 18

Index

Regina 111
Reid, Charles 146
Reid, Walter 85
Reveira, Frank 136
Richards, Henderson 142
Rita 82
Roach, Eric 143
Roach, Keith 119, 134-138
Roebuck Street 3, 64, 65, 80, 82, 91
Roett, Ishmael 140
Rogers, C.C. 41
Rogers, Herbert 41
Ronald Tree Cup 107, 117
Rowe, Mr 8
Rowe, Greg 146, 165
Royal Barbados Police Band 107
Royal Barbados Police Force 142
Rudder (Millward), Marcia 129

Salkeld, Thomas 9, 22
Salter, Hon Richard 3
Sandiford, Basil 143
Sandiford, Lloyd Erskine 121, 131
Sandiford, Dr Keith Albert 111-113, 147
Sandiford, Professor Keith A.P. 73, 85, 88, 130, 147
Sarjeant, Dudley 34, 45
Saskpower 111
'Sayer's Court' 58
Scott, Mrs Edna 129
Scott, Francis 85
Seale, Neilton 73, 94
Sealy, Arthur E. 105
Sealy, E.M. 38
Sealy, G. Harry 63, 65, 80, 108, 127-128, 133, 146
Sealy, J.E. Derek 55, 63-64, 65, 143
Sealy, Hon John 10
Sealy, Karl 143
Sealy, Philemon 161
Sealy, Philip 161
Sealy, Captain Rueben 45
Second World War 71, 100, 145
Seers, James 77
School uniforms 84
Scotland 34
Scouts Association of Barbados 40
Shepherd (First Combermerian Barbados Scholar) 111
Shilstone, E.M. 45
Simmons, Dr Erskine 147
Simmons, Keith 140

Skeete, E.B. (politician) 27
Skeete, E.B. (accountant) 29
Skeete, Patrick 83, 117, 146
Skinner, David 85
Skinner, Fred 65
Skinner, R. 125
Slave Rebellion (1816) 7
Slocombe, Gary 126
Small, the porter 136
Smith, C.E. Aurelius 104, 114
Smith, Denis 142
Smith, Neville LeR 88
Solomon, George 65
Somers Cox, Arthur 26, 27
Southwell, Victor A. 35, 40, 42, 49
Spartan Cricket Club 55
Speed, Rev Thomas Lyall 14-22, 23, 26, 43, 49, 55, 68, 72, 120, 143
Spooner's Hill 113
Springer, Charles Wilkinson 34, 39, 42, 47
Springer, Girwood 129
Springer, Sir Hugh 34, 121
St Andrew 11
St Ann's Cricket Club 55
St David's Church 14, 55
St Hill, Chalmer 65, 80-81, 139, 142
St John, Alfred 146, 165
St John, Bruce 65, 86, 118
St John, Sir Harold (Bernard) 121
St Lawrence Church 14
St Leonard's Boys' School 129
St Leonard's Girls' School 129
St Lucy 11, 28
St Margaret's Church 55
St Mary's Boys' School 8
St Michael 36
St Michael's Cathedral 73, 142
St Michael's Girls' School 46
St Michael's vestry 3, 4, 8, 9, 16, 17
St Simon's Chapel 11
Stella 82
Stroud, E.G. 38
Surrey 146
Swaby, Bishop W.P. 31
Swaby Commission (1907) 31-33, 53

Taitt, Brandford 140
Taitt, Eustace G. 77, 94
'Taxpayer' 25
Taylor, J.P. 34
Teachers' strike (1969) 105

177

Technical Institute 76
Theobalds, E.C.M. 87
Thomas, Frank G. 63
Thomas, Hon Grant E. 10
Thompson, David 140
Thornhill, Sir Timothy 3
Toppin, the porter 136
Toronto 147
Trinidad 104, 145
Trinidad & Tobago 164
Tucker, P.A.K. 90
Tudor, Sir James C. 78, 121
Turks & Caicos Islands 106

United Kingdom 86
United Lodge of the Masonic Body 7
United States of America 137
University College of Wales 69
University College of the West Indies 77, 88, 94, 98, 104, 122, 130
University of Toronto 78, 110

Vaughan, Hilton 37, 45, 140, 147, 151
Victoria Girls' School 28, 29
'Vindex' 71

Wade, Dr Carl 142
Walcott, Colonel 142
Walcott, Derek 143
Walcott, Francis S. 34, 39
Walcott, Frank 121
Walcott, Leslie A. 38
Wales 100
Walker, Cyril 140
Walker, Ralph 85
Walkes, Stirling 147
Walrond, Hon Thomas 3
Wanderers Cricket Club 53, 85
Wason, Harcourt 117, 146
Waterford 46, 61, 72, 78, 83, 84, 91, 93, 94, 95, 96, 99, 103-121, 127, 133
Weatherhead 34

Weatherhead, Bruce 34, 45, 143
Webster House 73
Webster, L.L. 'Goot' 35, 41, 49, 50, 57, 65, 73, 80
Weekes, Everton 85
Weekes, Lawson 140
Welfare Fund 83
West India Committee 65
West Indian Federation 101, 164
West Indies 13, 18, 22, 36, 46, 55, 63, 65, 79, 164
Weymouth 46, 60-61, 64, 80, 81, 83, 85, 91-92, 95
Weymouth Estate 3, 60
Weymouth House 73, 118
Wharton, Harold A. 129
White, Harold 142
Wickham, C.W. 'Billy' 65, 105
Wickham, Clennell Wilsden 64
Wickham, John 143
Wilkinson, Sam 129
Williams, Albert 145
Williams, E.A.V. 'Foffie' 55, 143
Williams, Clyde 129
Williams, Captain Francis 6
Williams, Captain Herbert 45
Williams, John 129
Williams, Lionel 85
Williams, Vincent 'Bull' 35, 39, 42, 49, 55, 57, 65, 80, 88, 95, 103, 146
Wilson, John 'Gladio' 15, 35, 49, 50, 53, 80, 95
Wiltshire, Mr 4
Winnipeg 146, 147
Wood, Bishop Wilfred 85, 147
Worrell, Sir Frank 63, 118, 143
Worrell, Lindsay 142
Worrell House 118
Wright, J.O. 27

Yarde, Calvin 'Archie' 94, 146, 165
YMCA 57